Praise for *The Unlikely Secret Agent*

'This is a wonderful book about a courageous and extraordinary woman who was highly principled, yet endowed by nature with all the clandestine skills. Her exploits recall the heroism of the great SOE (Special Operations Executive) women agents of the Second World War, yet the values she fought for so intrepidly are ___ in the balance today. Ronnie Kasrils tells her story with hum___ ride that the reader can only share.' – John le Carré

'Secret acts of great ___ ___en and women overthrew apartheid ___ ___ing, or a change of heart by the white regi___ ___. Eleanor Kasrils's amazing role in this story is told by ___ Ronnie for the first time. Readers of his earlier books will rec___ ___ the excitement of his storytelling and his memory for telling detail, but the tenderness of this book is new … Ronnie's response to Eleanor's sudden death last year at home in South Africa was to write this extraordinary book at breakneck speed. It is a love story, a historical document of great importance, and a terrific tale of a clandestine success.' – Victoria Brittain

'A moving tribute to a wonderful person truly an unlikely secret agent. It made me realise again just how much we owe to so many people for the freedom we enjoy in South Africa.' – Archbishop Desmond Tutu

'Fugitives, freedom fighters, lovers: *The Unlikely Secret Agent* is the remarkable true story of the South African liberation struggle's very own Bonnie and Clyde.' – John Carlin

'This is a deep and enduring love story that spans almost five decades, two large continents and the unromantic circumstance of a revolution waged in the face of transnational repression... All of it true and verifiable! – Trevor Manuel

'This is the story of Eleanor Kasrils, who showed great courage during her detention and escape, a woman of indomitable spirit and determination who refused to be browbeaten by the apartheid police. It is lovingly narrated by Ronnie Kasrils.' – Professor Kader Asmal

'Eleanor Kasrils was catapulted into the politics of the national democratic movement by the terrible events at Sharpeville and Langa of March 1960. Because her conscience would not allow her to stand by passively muttering complaints, she threw herself heart and soul into the struggle to eradicate racism and apartheid. That commitment led to her being cast in the unlikely roles of a burglar, saboteur, underground courier and ultimately that of exile. For twenty-seven years Eleanor and her husband Ronnie were engaged in some of the most clandestine aspects of the struggle for liberation. Leading a life filled with the tensions, anxieties and suspense typical of a spy thriller, Eleanor still was able to run a household and bring up two sons. Perhaps it was precisely her image, belying the work she was engaged in, that made her successful. This slim volume retells the story of one more dimension of our multifaceted liberation struggle that has remained secret till now.' – Z. Pallo Jordan

'This "little" book about an "ordinary" woman with the heart of a lioness confirms the truth that our freedom was not free. From its pages rings out another truth that among the outstanding heroines and heroes of the South African struggle were those who did not set out to perform heroic deeds. These are the heroic combatants for freedom like the Unlikely Secret Agent, Eleanor Kasrils, the subject of this engrossing "little book", who did the equally "little" things without which victory over the apartheid regime would have been impossible … Eleanor's story also poses a question about the future – what are the "little things" each one of us should do to win the new struggle for the further entrenchment of democracy and the defeat of poverty and underdevelopment, acting as our own liberators?' – Thabo Mbeki

The Unlikely Secret Agent

The Unlikely Secret Agent

by Ronnie Kasrils

MONTHLY REVIEW PRESS
New York

Originally published as *The Unlikely Secret Agent*
by Jacana Media (Pty) Ltd in 2010

Library of Congress Cataloging-in-Publication Data
        Kasrils, Ronald.
  The unlikely secret agent / by Ronnie Kasrils.
      p. cm.
  Originally published: Auckland Park, South Africa : Jacana Media, 2010.
  ISBN 978-1-58367-277-8 (pbk. : alk. paper) — ISBN 978-1-58367-304-1
(cloth : alk. paper) 1. Kasrils, Eleanor, 1936-2009. 2. Kasrils, Ronald.
3. African National Congress—Biography. 4. Anti-apartheid
activists—South Africa—Biography. 5. Apartheid—South Africa—History. 6.
South Africa—Social conditions—1961-1994. I. Title.
  DT1949.K37K37 2012
  968.06092—dc23
  [B]

                         2012007242

Monthly Review Press
146 West 29th Street, Suite 6W
New York, NY 10001
www.monthlyreview.org

5 4 3 2 1

For Eleanor, family and friends

Contents

Preface

This book covers four eventful years in the life of my wife, Eleanor Kasrils. We met in Durban in 1960 in the wake of the Sharpeville massacre and a year later became lovers. This was a dangerous and dramatic time in South African history. Eleanor was one of that rare breed of white South Africans who became actively involved in the liberation struggle against the apartheid system, at a time when the ANC-led Movement embarked on violent resistance. She was prepared to suffer the consequences. She did remarkable things with humour, verve and courage and engaged in a personal duel of wits with her brutal Security Police captors.

In retelling her story, I have striven to remain faithful to an account I heard her relate many times to myself, her children and friends. I have inevitably had to resort to my imagination in certain places but believe I have been true to the context and narrative which she vividly described and with which I was on the whole extremely well acquainted. It is a story that bears telling not only to South Africans, especially the younger generation who never knew what it was like to live in a police state, but to a wider readership. During the latter months of her life I said to Eleanor that we simply had to write the story together. Sadly it has been left to me alone to fulfil that wish.

Eleanor walking down West Street, Durban, in her Griggs bookstore uniform.

1

Eleanor's arrest on 19 August 1963 hit Durban's literary world like a bombshell. No one expected that the daughter of the manageress of Griggs, the city's best bookstore, and of a father who had a fine nose for an art deal, would be one of the first white women in the country to fall victim to the draconian detention laws that had just been passed by the National Party government.

She was diligently at work in her mother's bookstore when officers of the dreaded Security Branch (SB) strode into the premises to take her away for questioning. As the slender, young blonde saw Lieutenant Grobler bearing down on her, with an equally grim companion at his side, she dropped the books she had been sorting and made a run for it.

Suddenly a third man appeared, blocking her way, and lunged at her. She dodged him and, twisting and turning between rows of bookshelves, made a desperate dash for the rear exit. But her flight led her straight into the arms of a burly policeman with a clipped Hitler moustache, who had been stationed there as a back-stop. A couple of shop assistants cried out in astonishment.

The flushed Grobler caught up with her, cursing under his breath. 'Come, come, missis,' he said as he regained his composure. 'No need to bolt *soos 'n haas*. We just want to take you in for a cosy chat.'

As they led her towards the exit they found their way barred by a stern-looking woman. This was Helen Logan, Eleanor's mother and the shop's manageress, who had immigrated to South Africa in 1936 with her infant daughter. She was a strong-minded, no-nonsense Scot who did not tolerate fools gladly. Inflating her chest, which came naturally to her, she demanded to know what they thought they were doing.

'We're taking this lady off for questioning in terms of the country's Ninety-Day Detention Act,' Grobler explained, clearly irritated.

'And just what makes you think you can come into these premises on such an errand without first referring to management?' she huffed, suppressing her fears.

'Madam, under this new legislation, Act 37 of 1963, we cannot afford to alert a detainee as to our intentions,' Grobler responded, unsuccessfully attempting to push past her.

'Sir,' she stated, 'this young woman is not only in my employ, she happens to be my daughter, and I am sure she has done nothing to merit your intrusion here.'

'Well, Mrs Helen Logan, we'll see about that. We have our information and we act according to the law. All she needs do is answer a few questions satisfactorily at our office and, if so, I undertake that you will see her by tea-time.'

Helen Logan raised an eyebrow. The fact that the man was so familiar with her name was disconcerting. Given her daughter's strange comings and goings of recent months, she hesitated: 'Eleanor, can you do that?' Her tone was more an instruction than a question; she was used to being obeyed.

'Mom, don't believe them. These are evil men who will harm

me,' she protested as Grobler and his associates proceeded to usher her along. A young woman, barely out of her teens, who worked in the children's book section, attempted to intervene. Her face was livid and tearful and she grabbed Grobler's hands in an effort to break his grip. 'Damn it,' she cried out. 'You're hurting her. Can't you let her walk normally?'

For a small man, a foot shorter than the sturdy young woman, Grobler was able to sweep her aside with a flick of the hand as though she was a light weight.

As they bundled Eleanor into their Volkswagen – a car much loved by the Special Branch of the time – she attempted to cry out, 'This man's name is Grobler,' but it turned into a muffled cry as he covered her mouth with a freckled hand, the spots of which grew redder according to his mood swings.

Eleanor was relieved that her mother was aware of her arrest and knew she would immediately contact the family lawyer. She was thankful, too, that the young woman had seen them arresting her: she would inform mutual friends of the development. It also meant that her detention would get into the newspapers. That would put pressure on the police to charge or release her sooner rather than later. As they drove off she glimpsed the young woman running along the pavement waving anxiously. Grobler glanced at the receding figure and muttered to his partner, 'We must get that bloody *meisie's* name, damn troublemaker.'

'You leave her alone,' Eleanor remonstrated. 'She's just a kid out of school, horrified that you could just walk in and remove me like this. It's a natural response. She's not political.'

3

2

Eleanor expected the police to take her to their central city headquarters. Instead they drove through the busy morning traffic to the outskirts of the city and into a low-income suburb called Wentworth, where people of mixed race struggled to make ends meet. It was there she discovered that the Special Branch were operating from a new building and that it was being used as an interrogation centre.

'Dis ons Waarheids Huis [our House of Truth],' Grobler told her in Afrikaans, as they got out of the car. 'You tell us the truth, the whole truth, and nothing but the truth, missis, and you got a life.' He smirked. 'Don't try and fool with us, and spare yourself trouble. If you don't give us the information we require, I guarantee I will break you or hang you.'

The place was like a busy railway station in a war zone with passengers' destinations appearing to be to hell and back. About a dozen male detainees, looking as if they had been brought in from a battlefield, were slumped on wooden benches in a reception room. Some of them she recognised. A man in a maroon balaclava mask was pointing out one or two of them to a police officer.

As she was escorted through the building she saw an old African man being dragged down the stairs by a hulk of a policeman. Before she could recover from that shocking sight, a young friend of hers, Ebrahim Ismail Ebrahim, whom she had very recently helped hide, was being hauled out of an office unconscious. Down another passageway, she came across yet another young man with whom she had been on many protest demonstrations. He was a handsome fellow called Sonny Singh, but his face was now swollen from beatings. He managed a brave grin as they passed her. The effort caused him to begin spitting blood while she bit her lip in horror.

Before she knew it, she was shoved into a small office by Grobler with a crowd of yelling policemen swarming behind. They pressed in on her in the confined space, mean and angry. Her knees began to buckle as she tried to back away, only to find powerful arms propping her up from behind. She felt nauseous and vulnerable, with the blood throbbing through her temples and her breath coming in short, desperate gasps. It was as though she was drowning in a dark, heaving ocean. Though she could see them screaming and yelling, all she could hear was a roaring noise, and then, shrill and wild above the din, Grobler's grating voice, slapping into her with the force of a leather strap: 'I'll break you or hang you.'

He had her backed up against the wall, his hand on her throat. The room went quiet for a moment, and then the angry ocean tide poured in again. Pushed, pummelled, disorientated and well-nigh crushed into submission, she lost all sense of time. Suddenly she was shoved into a chair. Grobler was seated at a desk, while an associate took out a pen and notebook and the other males crowded round, glassy eyes drilling into her.

The man with the pad asked her whether her boyfriend, Ronnie Kasrils, was a Jew. The room was silent. With her mind spinning furiously, she seemed to have sailed drunkenly away from her body. Was she hearing correctly?

The man repeated the question and Grobler watched her intently. She felt utterly disembodied. As the words sank in, she blinked, wondering whether this was real or some horrible nightmare. As she struggled to comprehend what was happening, she wondered whether she should bother to answer what was an insulting and strange demand.

Why all this fuss to determine whether Ronnie was Jewish? There was no secret about the matter although he was not religious – being what was called 'a practising Jew'. She knew that if she answered even a simple question she could be drawn into answering many more and so she kept a defiant silence. The man with the pad asked again: 'Is Kasrils a Jew? Is Ronnie Kasrils a bloody Jew?'

Suddenly she became conscious of the heavy mist lifting from her mind, and she flared up, defiant and unintimidated. 'You have a nerve to ask a question like that after the way you've been manhandling me.' She turned angrily on Grobler: 'You said at the bookshop, to me and to my mother, that all you wanted was to take me in for a few questions. Is this the way the Special Branch asks questions? And the beatings going on in this Gestapo centre – you're torturing people here. One day you're going to have to answer for this. Whether I get out dead or alive, you are going to be exposed, mark my words.'

There was laughter and jeering. Another policeman spoke, Malan, the burly man with the Hitler moustache: 'Lady, you know about the Rivonia raid last month and all the Jews involved with Mandela and his gang: Arthur Goldreich, Lionel Bernstein, Denis Goldberg, Harold Wolpe. And now Kasrils pops up here. We smell a Jewish conspiracy with the

6

kaffirs, to give this country to the bloody communists.'

Good grief, she thought, this was unreal. These people are really serious about determining Ronnie's religion as though it would help prove a ridiculous conspiracy theory of their making.

Grobler had been silently following every word. 'Look, missis, this is no trivial matter,' he started. 'Do you think it's a coincidence that all these people belong to the Goldreich–Slovo clan? Virtually all their lawyers are Jews – Maisels, Chaskalson, Joel Joffe.' He said something vulgar in Afrikaans to his colleagues, about *'n Jood se piel*, and they all laughed uproariously.

'We want you to confirm whether he's a Jew,' Grobler demanded, thumping the desk. 'Is he a Jew?'

'Lieutenant Grobler,' Eleanor answered in an icy tone, 'I don't have to be Sherlock Homes to suggest that you check his birth certificate.'

Grobler went red in the face and a nerve twitched under a yellow-green eye. Leaning forward he leered at her: 'Tell me, missis, is your man circumcised?'

There was a long silence. Eleanor sat with folded arms, disgust written on her face, and looked at the floor. Grobler began thumping the desk again.

'Where is Kasrils? Where is the Jewboy? Where is he hiding?' He kept pounding away, over and over. She sat biting her tongue, digging her nails into her palms, her contempt for Grobler evident in her stony expression.

At that point there came a more friendly voice – one of the older Special Branch men, Wessels, who had once taken her name at a City Hall demonstration. He had the

7

courteous demeanour of the old-school Afrikaner. 'You really ought to help yourself by co-operating with us. There are strong indications that you've been deeply involved in secret activities against the government, not just minor protest demonstrations in public, by allowing Kasrils to involve you in sabotage operations. You know that if you just give us Kasrils's whereabouts, you'll be let off the hook. Give yourself a break.'

His polite tone was inviting. She was desperate to have him take over from Grobler and knew it would most likely happen if she responded positively to him. But instead she shook her head and covered her eyes, moist with tears. There was silence. She was breathing slowly and deeply, giving herself time to think. His remark that she had been involved in Ronnie's sabotage activity worried her. Under no circumstances would she react to that. As time ticked by, she remained silent.

Wessels tried again, with the same line of encouragement, the same seductive questions. After a while she looked directly into his eyes. 'Lieutenant Wessels,' she said with quiet dignity, 'I've come to know you as an officer doing your job not because you like to demean people but because you strive to be professional in your own way. I know from the older Congress people, black and white, that from the time of the 1956 Treason Trial you raided and arrested and gave evidence in court but never lied or used force or abused any of them. And here you are now, the good cop facilitating the work of this vicious upstart, Grobler, who's no credit to your force.'

Wessels shrugged his shoulders and shifted slightly uneasily in his seat. Grobler screeched at her in fury: 'No lectures, missis. You're in the hot seat!'

3

They grilled her all day. The team was led by Grobler, while Wessels simply acted as a back-seat observer. Eleanor noted that Grobler kept swallowing pills, possibly to curb high blood pressure, and indeed his face would become crimson at times with anger. From the line of questioning she realised that they knew far too much of the underground's operations for her good.

'Who apart from Kasrils visited the bookshop for messages and money?'

'You ordered Che Guevara's book on guerrilla warfare. Who did you give copies to? We want every name.'

'When Kasrils and Billy Nair broke into the dynamite store, who gave them the key for the outside gate?'

'Who did you see in Johannesburg when you travelled there with reports and returned with funds? Who were the Jews there?'

To all of this she looked back blankly. The hours went by. When she said she needed to go to the toilet, she was surprised that they agreed. She had heard that they would often deliberately humiliate grown men by leaving them to wet themselves. When they allowed her to go twice that morning to the toilet, she realised they were uneasy about causing discomfort to a female – all except Grobler, who said, 'Can't

9

you damn well wait?' But no, she said, she could not, and even he begrudgingly relented. These visits gave her the chance to recover her composure and assess the situation.

As she was escorted along the corridor the second time, one of the office doors had been left ajar. Glancing in, she was surprised to see a senior underground member calmly smoking a cigarette. A maroon balaclava mask lay on the desk before him. It was Bruno Mtolo, whom she had worked with very closely. When he saw her he cast his eyes down and she sensed at once that he was co-operating with the SB. It had been three weeks since they captured him and he looked remarkably fit. The message was clear: co-operate and things will be OK; resist and face a hammering.

Back in the interrogation room she realised they had let her see Bruno on purpose. 'Your friend Bruno's singing like a canary,' Grobler boasted. 'It will save him from the noose. He'll give evidence in court, you'll see, and he'll get off scot-free. We didn't even have to lay a hand on him. He's a clever kaffir. Knows what's good for him. Came to an understanding with us within twenty-four hours of his capture. Sang like a little yellow canary.'

Wessels again spoke up. 'We know that you and Kasrils were close to Bruno Mtolo. He was rising high up the ranks. You believe all these people are of high morality like Chief Luthuli, Walter Sisulu or your friend Billy Nair. Forget it. We can tell you that Bruno Mtolo has been in prison many times for robbery. He's a criminal who joined the trade union movement when it was convenient. He is petrified of going back to prison and is ready to sell you all out. There's no point in resisting.'

10

Eleanor's mind was racing. She knew how impressed Billy and Ronnie had been when they broke into the dynamite store and Bruno had so skilfully jemmied open the safes in which the explosives were stored. No one then wondered where he had acquired the ability. Maybe he *was* a former convict. That would explain his skills. But then again, maybe Wessels was lying about Bruno – perhaps even setting him up. The maroon mask could easily have been placed on the table to give the impression that he was the man she had seen pointing out comrades in the reception area. The underground gave guidance about what to expect under interrogation and she had been warned that one of the Security Branch's tricks was to claim that other comrades were talking. Maybe he had smoked a cigarette, but was that adequate proof? She was unsure, and yet the embarrassment evident in Bruno's eyes was real enough.

Grobler again reiterated that he did not want much from her: just to tell them where her boyfriend was hiding. 'That Jew who's left you in the lurch. That Jew, Ronnie Kasrils.' He kept repeating the name, accentuating the first 's' and drawing out the latter part of the surname so that the pronunciation sounded like a hissing snake uncoiling. 'Ronnie Kasssrillls, who like all Jewboys uses you Christian girls for sexual pleasure. Not so, missis? But they never marry you in the end,' he snapped. 'They only marry their own kind, you see. But that's right, missis. People should stick to their own kind, not so? That's natural: white with white, Jew with Jew, coolie with coolie, kaffir with kaffir.'

He nodded sagely as though he was delivering a lecture in sociology. 'I suppose you're just mesmerised,' he added, 'drowning in a sexual whirlpool. It's because he's circumcised, isn't it, missis?'

That stung her. 'Don't you dare speak to me like that!' She knew Wessels would not support such an approach. Grobler was a new boy, transferred from the murder and robbery squad, which was known for breaking hardened criminals through torture, and she sensed an old-timer like Wessels would be none too happy with an upstart brought in over his head. She knew they would hold a post-mortem after interrogation sessions, and disagreements among them over tactics employed could work in her favour.

Late in the afternoon there was just Grobler with her in the office, which was pungent with male hormones. He started on his line of questioning again, in a disturbingly quiet but tight voice. 'Where is he? Where is your boyfriend? We know you know. Come on, just tell me and you can go home. Your child must be wondering where you are.'

The reference to her seven-year-old daughter, Brigid, unsettled her. She chewed her lip and looked away, feeling exhausted and afraid. Thankfully the little girl was being looked after by her parents.

He could see she was afraid, and indeed he wanted her that way. He instantly cut back to his main line of inquiry. 'You're still hiding him, aren't you? Where?' he asked, the menace rising in his voice. She stared him down, showing her resolve again.

Grobler became infuriated, uncontrollable anger welling up within him. He despised this *Engelse vrou* – like her mother, full of superior airs and graces, working with books and in love with a damned Jew.

12

'Is it his circumcised prick that excites you?' He leant over her, shaking her violently, aroused by his own babbling and by her palpable fear and vulnerability, which ignited his sense of power. 'You bitch!' he began yelling, his spit flying into her face. 'I'll break you or hang you!' He grabbed her hair and banged her head on the table.

Eleanor screamed for help. The sweat was streaming down his face, which had turned scarlet again. It was all he could do to stop himself from beating her with his fists as he shook her by the neck until she blacked out.

She came to, sobbing. Some of the other policemen were back in the room. Wessels offered her a glass of water; he appeared embarrassed. Grobler had disappeared. She asked what manner of beast was he, telling Wessels that the police had never behaved like that before. Though flustered, she was angry and brave enough to go on the offensive.

After an hour Grobler returned. He had freshened up and was drawing deep on a cigarette, casually blowing smoke rings her way, as if to emphasise how much he was in control.

'Missis,' he told her in an official voice, as though nothing unusual had transpired and everything was perfectly normal, 'since you have failed to co-operate, I have authority to hold you under the Ninety-Day Sabotage Act – Act 37 of 1963 – and we will be taking you to detention cells. In terms of the Act,' he continued, 'it is not incumbent on the state to formulate a charge against you. You will be kept in solitary confinement for ninety days. You have no right to see a lawyer, and no right to a trial unless we deem it so. If you fail to co-operate with us in that period, if you fail to provide us with the true answers to our questions, we have the right to re-detain you for a further ninety days. And if we want to, we will throw away the key.'

Eleanor's heart skipped a beat as Grobler announced her fate. But she was determined to conceal her fear. She demanded a chance to see her parents to make sure they would look after her daughter. Grobler was straining to speak calmly and she could see his jaw muscles grinding with the effort.

'You see, missis,' he said tightly, 'you make trouble, you mix with this communist, this Jewboy, he leaves you to face the music and now you are left alone to worry about your little girl.'

He paused for effect. 'Don't worry, missis, we Afrikaners care about children. We will take care of her for you. We will find a good home for her, decent people who will bring her up properly, in a true God-fearing way, so that she knows all about the evils of communism.'

Eleanor exploded. 'Don't you dare talk about my daughter that way! I'm going to see my lawyers and report you for assault.' To which he laughed. 'No access under the Ninety-Day Act, no access to lawyers, hey!' And he leaned over grinning triumphantly through yellow teeth. She could smell the liquor on his breath. Though it nauseated her, it also gave her the hope that if she curbed her fear of physical assault, she could get the better of him.

He allowed her the telephone call. When her father answered, he asked in a strained, far-off voice how she was. He told her the whole town was talking about her arrest that morning and that their lawyers were taking the matter up at the highest level. 'Dad, please take care of Brigid,' she said. When she told him they were keeping her in detention under the Ninety-Day Act, he broke down and sobbed pitifully. At that point Grobler cut them off.

14

4

Eleanor was driven back through the city. When they arrived at Durban Central Prison, her heart sank because it was not the kind of place you felt you could escape from. Ninety-day detainees were instructed by the Movement to sit out their detention and, as a relatively new, disciplined member, Eleanor would have been ready to comply. But the instruction had already proved to be totally impractical as many cadres broke under interrogation and others had been accepting one-way visas into exile.

The shock of realising that someone as senior and trusted as Bruno Mtolo was in all likelihood co-operating made her realise that there would be plenty of evidence for the police to stage court trials when it suited them and obtain convictions – possibly even death sentences. The thought made her shudder.

She was ushered in through a small doorway within the massive outer doors. The prison was dank and cold in the autumn evening, particularly for a subtropical city like Durban, and she was glad for the light cardigan she had on. At first the small female section appeared hollow and empty but then she heard shrill babbling emanating from behind a cell door. A tough-looking wardress, with heavy make-up and peroxided blond hair, told her in a frosty way: 'Those are ladies of the night, cooling off. You're a VIP. You have a room to yourself. No view. This is not the Edward Hotel.'

She was placed in a small, gloomy cell with a double bunk-bed and a pile of filthy grey blankets. A cracked basin and foul-smelling toilet with a broken seat completed the furnishings. The surroundings did not bother her so much, for she had already spent the odd night in police cells after the break-up of protest demonstrations. During previous arrests she had been in the company of other women, who always sang to keep their spirits up. There was a song that particularly appealed to her, 'Malibongwe', which praised the commitment of women. On completion it would be followed by the chant 'Once you have touched a woman you have struck a rock!' On such occasions the companionship was a tremendous source of strength. But being detained in isolation was another matter entirely. Isolation played on the mind, nagged at one's weaknesses, brought out one's demons. Could she last ninety days? Those responsible for the new law understood human psychology only too well. She felt dreadfully alone.

The peroxided blonde came in with a cold stare and an equally cold meal of stringy mutton and glassy potatoes, which Eleanor toyed with. She knew she would not be able to sleep much. The long night, with shrieks and shrill voices from the cell down the passage; the unfathomable rattling of iron doors; the sound of crying which made her hold her breath for she kept imagining it was her daughter; all left her battling to calm herself and think clearly.

Her mind whirled from one thought to the other, striving to understand exactly what the police knew; how to resist giving away sensitive information; especially how to safeguard Ronnie, for whose life she desperately feared; how to conceal

16

the identities of the Johannesburg leaders upon whom so much depended. She was worried because she realised that she knew far too much. She couldn't bear to think of the repercussions should she crack. Then there was the need to inform the underground that Bruno was probably talking, so that they could take the necessary precautions.

Above all, she was disturbed by the threats to her daughter though the knowledge that her parents would take care of the child consoled her. She was restless and every so often jumped up from the discomfort and musky odour of the bunk to pace up and down the cell. She fiddled for ages with the metal springs under the mattress and began prising some loose, deciding they might be useful for picking the door lock. She was seething with anger at the manner in which Grobler had treated her and decided that if there appeared no hope of early release she would resort to a hunger strike. She and Ronnie had discussed such eventualities and had concluded that even at the worst of times one must fight the depression of defeat and, by working on a plan, form a positive response.

So she resolved not to answer any questions; to go on a hunger strike owing to her unjust detention; and to work on an escape plan. With that, her mind stopped its uncontrollable contortions and she settled down somewhat.

After a night in which she dozed on and off, the wardress opened her cell and slammed an enamel mug of tea and plate of porridge on the floor. When she ordered Eleanor to turn up her mattress and saw that some metal springs had been removed and then found them under a pile of unused blankets, she was furious. 'Are you making a weapon? Are you trying to escape? I'm reporting you to Lieutenant Grobler when he comes. He'll fix your fancy arse!'

In a deliberate move Eleanor kicked the plate of food and mug away. The wardress did a double-take, blinking in astonishment. *Goeie griet*, she thought, as she momentarily raised her hand to slap her but thought better of it, how do you threaten someone with worse punishment when they are already so deep in trouble? Even she was in awe of the immense powers that detention without charge and solitary confinement under the new Act gave the Security Police. 'Clean that up at once,' she barked out, 'or there'll be no food when you get back tonight!'

'Good!' Eleanor answered in a calm, level voice, which gave added weight to her resolve. 'I don't want your rotten food anyway. Tell them I'm on a hunger strike because I'm being unjustly detained.'

5

When Grobler arrived he was in a blind rage. 'You bitch!' he screamed. 'What do you think you're doing?'

He began shaking her roughly. Again he pulled her hair and started throttling her. This time she pretended to black out and collapsed in a heap. She heard them running about in a panic and then she was doused with a bucket of water. She allowed the tears to surface and began crying. She found this easy to do, and genuine tears rolled uncontrollably down her face. Grobler tried to pacify her. 'Missis,' he pleaded, 'get a grip on yourself. Pull yourself together!' He was trying to stir her. 'The sooner you calm down, the sooner we can take you for questioning. The sooner we get satisfactory answers, the sooner we release you and you can see your daughter.'

'Pull yourself together!' The words echoed in her head. She loathed and detested being spoken to in that way. That was how the Catholic sisters at the convent school used to berate her when she was stubborn. That was how her ex-husband used to speak to her when she began rebelling against his manner of ordering her about. She had in fact pulled herself together, but not in the way he expected, for she walked out on him after five years with her child and clothes and little else.

She thought of that time in her life and how she had won the battle for independence, despite even her parents' protestations, from a marriage that had come to suffocate her. The thought of that victory strengthened her, fortified her more than the tips she had been given by the Movement about how to cope with detention and interrogation. They were useful: like calming down to allow yourself to assess the situation; breathing deeply and evenly to remain calm; knowing that they would promise to release you in exchange for informing on others; knowing they would boast that almost everyone else was talking; the playing of the good-cop bad-cop routine to soften you up. But her own life experience was even more valuable.

She managed to break free of Grobler's grip and glared at him. She was frightened no longer. 'Don't you dare lay a finger on me again, you coward,' she snapped at him, her eyes burning like embers, and he appeared to shrink a little. It seemed she was getting some control over the process and realised they were a little out of their comfort zone in dealing with her.

6

Back at the Wentworth House of Truth that second day, the interview was attended by a senior policeman, who was introduced as Major Frans Steenkamp. He watched quietly while Grobler and Malan, the burly one, handled the interrogation.

'Come, missis, tell us what you know about the theft of dynamite at the Pinetown store,' Grobler demanded. She stared back blankly. 'Come on,' he continued. 'Kasrils took you with, when he reconnoitred the place. We know that from Bruno Mtolo. We know he later opened the dynamite safes once they were in the compound. But Kasrils had a key to the outer gate. Where did he get that key? How did he get it? Who gave it to him?'

'Come on, lady,' Malan started. 'Help yourself, and we will drop charges against you. Who drove the get-away car, the blue Ford, when Kasrils and his team dynamited the electric pylons? Whose car was that? Kasrils does not have a car, we know that. We know more than you think. We'll get these answers from others. We'll get everything in the end. Just admit it all and save us and yourself the trouble. There's no point in being stubborn,' he urged as though they were doing her a favour.

'This is serious trouble, missis,' Grobler cut in sharply.

'Dynamiting pylons – your boyfriend's speciality. That's a very serious charge. We have the evidence. Your people are singing like canaries. The whole of Natal was plunged into darkness. Do you realise how much the economy suffered that time?'

'And then,' Malan chimed in again, 'there's the matter of the bomb at the Central Post Office last Christmas. That was dangerous. People could have been killed, you know. Only whites could have been there that time of night. Was that Kasrils?'

'And what about the bomb at our satellite office in Baker Street? Some officers working late had just left. If they had remained a little longer they would have died. That's a hanging charge. Who did that, missis? It could only have been whites, free to move around in the centre of the city that late.' Grobler went on incessantly and the others all seemed to lean in on her. A bomb at one of their own offices: that riled them.

Eleanor struggled to keep a clear head. Bruno knew a great deal about Ronnie's involvement as far as preparation and training were concerned and had shown them the dynamite site, but to her knowledge he had only been on one earlier operation with Ronnie. He knew far less about her involvement other than that she had participated in the reconnaissance of the dynamite site. Sure, she and Ronnie had enjoyed his company – his sense of humour, his easy laugh, his technical know-how and skill – but they had come to have their doubts about his reliability early on owing to his heavy bouts of drinking. On one occasion they had taken him to a party, one of those mixed-race affairs where the booze ran freely. He had drunk non-stop, fallen into a stupor and wet his pants. From that time on they had kept him in the dark as far as possible. In fact she felt Ronnie had been protecting her from him.

Suddenly she recalled the night when she and Ronnie had

approached the Security Police office in Baker Street by way of a back lane, carrying explosives in a small bag. Someone had been passing by and appeared suspicious. To conceal what they were up to, he had drawn her into his arms and began kissing her passionately – just two lovers in the shadows. For a moment she felt miles away with him, hoping she would wake up from this nightmare and find herself lying in his arms.

Major Steenkamp spoke. He was a suave, authoritative man of higher social station than the others. He was new, too, for she had been involved in protest politics for two years and had got to know the Special Branch regulars – older men like Wessels – a breed from a less menacing time. Clearly the state had begun to deploy new crack detectives to the Security Branch in an effort to deal with the growing sabotage campaign unleashed by the Mandela–Sisulu leadership.

Steenkamp addressed her politely in a clipped English accent: 'Madam, you must understand that my men have important work to do. Their task is nothing more nor less than the defence of state security. The methods now might be more robust, shall I say, than in the past. But I am afraid that you people have brought this on yourselves. Our job is to uphold law and order for the safety of our country and people, and the new law is simply to assist us to deal with this criminal violence which is in nobody's interest, white or black.'

Everyone listened carefully. The only sound was of Grobler's chair creaking as he rocked back and forth.

'You people have been literally and figuratively playing with dynamite and have forced us to take off the gloves,' Steenkamp continued, in his tight but courteous tone. 'Believe me, we are not too happy about this. But do you not realise that you are

24

being used by the communists – people like Ronald Kasrils? I have nothing against him for being a Jew. There are decent Jews who we do business with, buy our vehicles from, purchase our office furniture from at good prices.

'But this man is bad news for you. I am sure your parents will agree. Why is it that there are so many Jews in the communist party of this and other democratic countries? It is disturbing. Just look at how many were involved with Sisulu at the Rivonia headquarters. Slovo, too, only he got out of the country in time, leaving his wife and children behind. Now Kasrils – another Jew – has got you into the mess you are in. He would desert you for sure. You have helped him escape from us, first from your home here in Durban, then more recently from your parents' property up in Kloof. We know you arranged for him and his accomplices to hide out at that derelict place without your parents' knowledge.

'We know all about that. We know you kept your parents in the dark. But do you realise that if we wanted to, we could even pull *them* in? I mean, there were terrorists on their property. Let them prove their innocence in a court of law. Who then would look after your child?

'I do not threaten you. I simply spell out the situation you face, one of your own making, and the dire consequence should you not co-operate with us. Because, madam, it seems to me that you act with no thought of the consequences. In the end we are simply doing our job. Please do not play games with us anymore. We know everything. We have defeated the ANC and the Communist Party and their desperate attempt to derail the country with this sabotage campaign, with these senseless bombings that would end up killing people wholesale. Where has it got them? Mandela, Sisulu, Mbeki, Kathrada, Goldberg, Bernstein? They're all under lock and key. In time they'll face trial and, believe me, it could be the rope for them.

'They're finished. It's clearly over. Why should a minnow like you suffer with the big fish? You've made a mistake. You can go back to your little daughter, your parents, your job. We will say it was all a mistake. You can have the fine life back. Go and enjoy the beach, the fine restaurants, the dinner parties. Isn't that where you come from? We know you're fond of the art scene, the jazz clubs, the ballet, the film club. Your parents are socialites. Enjoy the kind of life that was meant for you. Pull back from the precipice Kasrils has dragged you to. You don't belong with the ANC and the communists. All I am asking is that you help us a little. Just give us a hint. Where can we find him?'

He peered at her, smooth and grim, a handsome man surrounded by his bloodhounds, she thought, sounding so reasonable. 'Just think of it this way. If you lead us to Kasrils you can help him give up quietly and he will be under arrest but safe. If not, we will get him in the end. That's inevitable and just a matter of time. You have both his fate and your fate in your hands. He will go down under gunfire. Mark my words. Your duty must be to save him.'

Silence. She bowed her head and stared at the floor, biting her lip, craving a cigarette. A refined young woman, with exceptional blue-grey eyes that glared at them in cold fury every time they spoke and seemingly turned to steel. She appeared so thin and frail, yet was so steadfast.

Grobler's chair went on squeaking. Silence. Steenkamp

rose slowly to depart. 'Think carefully. The ball is in your court. If you want to talk, just ask for me.'

'A moment, Major,' she requested. He looked down at the young woman. Had she at last succumbed? They waited for the anticipated capitulation they had often seen happen before.

'Just three points,' she said in a quiet voice. 'First, I am making it perfectly clear that I will not eat because of the injustice of my arrest. I will remain on hunger strike until you either charge me or release me.

'Second, I am laying an official complaint with you against Lieutenant Grobler for his indecent line of questioning. And everyone here is witness to that.

'Third, this same Grobler has manhandled me now on numerous occasions, both here and at Durban Central. And that's an official complaint too.'

'Madam,' he responded icily, 'not eating will harm nobody but yourself, and I urge you not to do so. I would hate to see you being force-fed with a tube down your throat. It's not a pretty sound or sight.

'As for your complaints, they must be backed up by witnesses. I apologise for any indecent questions, which will not be repeated. And there will be no rough stuff either. But understand, you are linked to violent action against the state, seditious activities, and as I have told you already, we have every reason to take the gloves off. I will not tie the hands of my men. I repeat again: you can extricate yourself from this discomfort by assisting us with our investigations. The ball is in your court.'

With that he left like a shadow.

7

'You'd better eat something,' Wessels advised her conciliatorily. 'I am leaving with the Major, but I'll tell the men to bring you something from the canteen. Not eating will affect your judgement and make you ill. Better eat.'

They brought her a hamburger and soggy chips with a Coke and left her alone. She took a small sip of the drink and ignored the food. When they got back they enquired why she was not eating.

'I repeat again: I will not eat because of this unjust detention and I will not eat until you charge or release me,' she announced emphatically. 'You've heard me telling your boss that.'

Grobler arrived. He had a gleam in his eyes and his face was flushed. He was seething with resentment. He ordered his men to clear out. Wessels had already gone. He thrust his face into hers. She smelt the liquor on his breath and realised he must secretly imbibe when he took a break.

'You think you're clever, missis, telling tall stories to the Major. You think I care? You heard him: if you want to lay a charge against me, find your witnesses. You think you can stop me executing my duty? Well, as the Lord is my witness, you will see: I'm going to break you, you bitch. Break you or hang you!'

He lifted her bodily out of the chair and slammed her into the wall, knocking the breath out of her. He banged her head several times whilst she groaned in agony, trying to fight him off. He was a tough man and hurled her to the floor where she collapsed in a heap. He jumped on her, pressing his pelvis obscenely into hers.

'Where is he, the bloody Jew?' he screeched. She kept hitting his chest to no avail. It was like being in the embrace of a wild animal. He turned from her, leaving her sobbing in a heap, and sat down to smoke.

They were both breathing hard. At first she fought to control herself and regain composure. But then she changed her mind. Once she started to cry, the tears, the frustration, the desperation took over and she could not stop.

She could see that even an appeal to Steenkamp about Grobler's behaviour meant nothing. Steenkamp's manner of playing things according to the book, of being prepared to take a complaint, was a mere charade. Grobler was a law unto himself. So she decided to sob, determined that they would not shut her up.

'For Christ sake, will you stop your blabbering!' Grobler snarled. She turned up the volume. He gave up and left the office in a fury. She stood up and threw the plate of food at the door, then grabbed a chair and began smashing it against the wall. As they rushed in to subdue her, she held a broken leg threateningly. She raised it to Grobler, who backed away. 'Don't let that bastard near me. He's a dirty old man,' she snarled, her eyes blazing as they circled her.

With two of them holding her, Grobler advanced with a pair of handcuffs. 'Enough of this,' he declared and snapped them on her wrists so that she winced. He sat her in a chair. 'I'll put you in a straitjacket if I have to,' he threatened. She buried her head in her arms and sobbed quietly and steadily. They offered her water and a cigarette, which she reluctantly declined. She thought of Bruno: smoking in their presence signalled co-operation.

The burly one with the Hitler moustache, Malan, tried to reason. 'Lady, just think of the Major's words. He gave you a way out of this mess. Why suffer unnecessarily? Remember he said to send for him the moment you want to talk.'

'Yes,' she responded quietly. 'As I said: tell him I'm on a hunger strike and that despite his words Grobler has actually assaulted me now – virtually the moment he left.'

'Jy lieg! Jy lieg!' Grobler screamed. 'That's a blue-faced lie. Bring your witnesses!'

8

The interrogation was over for the day. She felt dirty and humiliated but kept telling herself that it was they who were filthy. Malan drove her back to prison accompanied by another policeman. But instead of taking her straight there, they drove her home, saying she could pick up some clothes and toiletries. She thought they were trying to placate her.

She had been living with Ronnie in a small, single-bedroom cottage on the Florida Road, which ran up to the Berea heights above the sparkling city and harbour, not far from her parents' elegant home where her daughter, Brigid, was safe for the time. She and Ronnie had only recently moved into the cottage so she could be close to her daughter, whom she had been leaving more and more with her parents. It was a convenient arrangement, owing to her increased involvement in underground activity and particularly her need to travel now and then at weekends as a secret courier to Johannesburg. It had also become a wise option, she and Ronnie reasoned, because of the risks involved.

The cottage was in darkness. They had confiscated her keys and now opened up.

Her mind went back to the time just two months previously when they had swooped in the middle of the night to arrest him. Raids and arrests had been expected throughout the country under the new Ninety-Day Detention Act. The old guard, people like Billy Nair and others, wanted to brazen it out, rather than go underground. They had grown tired of that life. Meanwhile, the new generation of members were pressing for the necessity and adventure of clandestine operations on the run. But without permission from the leadership, Ronnie had held back against her pleadings and had not disappeared.

It was she who had insisted that they at least take precautions to avoid arrest. She had reminded him of a trap door in the floor which they had noted when they first moved in. It led nowhere but into the foundations of the house. They had placed their bed, which was box-like and legless, over it. When they dragged it aside and opened the trap door, it led into a cavity under the floorboards. The two of them cleared out the cobwebs and practised dragging the bed back and forth over the escape hatch. Though it was a heavy object, she managed to do it by herself.

When the dreaded late-night knock on the front door came some weeks later, sending their heart-beats racing, she was out of bed in a flash. With the knocking increasing in intensity, she helped him pull the bed aside so that he could slip through.

It was Grobler and Malan who presented themselves when she opened the front door. They told her they wanted to talk to Kasrils. When she said he was not there, they pushed past her and marched swiftly through the small living room, kitchen, bedroom and bathroom. They could see she was alone. They glanced about, looked under a table and in a couple of cupboards, but paid no attention to the bed. It seemed there could be nothing but flooring under it. She sat on the edge, her long legs comfortably crossed under her, and coolly fielded their questions, trembling inwardly while dragging on a cigarette. Where was he? When would he be back?

She pointed out a framed Freedom Charter signed by Chief Albert Luthuli, President of the banned ANC, and other leaders. It was the Movement's vision adopted at a mass rally in 1955 and declared that 'South Africa belongs to all who live in it, black and white, and that no government can justly claim authority unless it is based on the will of the people'. It had pride of place on her wall, but had accidentally fallen, damaging its frame.

'I will not be seeing him again,' she told them. 'I've had him and his politics. See that Freedom Charter? I hit him on the head with it.' They listened impassively and left, asking her to tell him to contact them the next day should he come by.

After what she thought was a safe interval, she helped Ronnie ease out through the trap door. He quickly dressed and made ready to get away. It was cold and dark outside. Eleanor had the presence of mind to first look out of the front door and saw in the nick of time the police Volkswagen parked down the road with two figures keeping watch on the house. Fortunately they had not spotted anything suspicious – just a frightened woman in a night-gown looking out at the street as if wondering whether her man was coming home. He immediately slipped back through the trap door and lay beneath the floorboards until first light while she passed down mugs of coffee to keep him warm and alert.

At last she heard the Volkswagen motor firing up and watched them drive away. Ronnie had to hurry now in case a replacement car and team were on the way. She told him to let her go out first as a decoy. They might have left someone behind to maintain surveillance. She would walk to a telephone booth down the road and pretend to make a call. If the coast was clear he could slip away.

At the booth she spent several minutes pretending to speak on the telephone. When she got back to the cottage, he was gone.

9

Now, just three months after that raid but seemingly a lifetime later, she was back at the cottage, which the Security Branch had ransacked. Books and clothing lay in untidy piles everywhere. The police had not, however, moved the bed and were obviously none the wiser about the trap door.

They showed her a pile of books including two copies of Che Guevara's book on guerrilla warfare. They said they were banned and would be confiscating them. When they told her she could be charged for having banned literature, she countered this by saying they could have been planted in her absence. 'Well,' Malan responded, 'this one by Che Guevara clearly has the sticker of your bookshop affixed. And no doubt you placed the order.'

'Those copies were ordered before the book was banned in this country, so show me what law I have contravened.' She was enjoying the exchange and added, 'I am glad to hear you talking about the law, because in a civilised country it gives an accused the right to a trial and defence lawyers. Your government has undermined the rule of law with this new Act.'

They did not respond to her nor to her complaints about the mess they had made. She tried see whether it was possible to leave a surreptitious note for her father, but when she fiddled with a pencil they took it from her. They did not see her niftily pocket a ten rand note. They allowed her to take a few essential toiletries and articles of clothing, but not the photograph of her child, and were set to depart.

She was worried that her carefully nurtured potted plants on the small veranda needed watering. When she asked whether she could attend to them, she was surprised at how readily they agreed. Nor did they try to hurry her up when she watered the plants and fussed over them, removing some dried leaves and a few snails feeding on the greenery. She regarded the snails as pests and normally waged relentless war to eliminate them. After the brutality she had sustained, she removed them gently and dropped them into a bush. Besides, she did not want to expend any kind of violence whatsoever on such placid creatures in the policemen's presence.

On the drive back to the prison they began to play games with her. She realised why they had been in no hurry. As they turned a corner, Malan's partner shouted hoarsely, 'There's Kasrils. Daar's hy!' Malan turned the car violently and they careered off, chasing a vehicle that had driven by. They overtook it and swerved past at high speed. 'No, he is in the car ahead, man!' and they sped like mad after it, screeching around corners so that she was thrown violently from side to side. They kept this game up for an hour. 'We will catch him, lady. We are hot on his trail.' It seemed a pathetic game but she said nothing.

They motored down from the Berea, along the Umgeni River to a beauty spot where the river entered the sea. This was a popular recreation area and Eleanor had often fished there as a girl with her father. He had been an engineer, apprenticed on the Clyde, and for a time worked, like his Scots father before him, on the Durban railways. He had nurtured the practical abilities she possessed, her skill in baiting their hooks, looking after the fishing tackle, checking electric cables in the home, changing the tyres on a car. She remembered those halcyon fishing trips which had done much to mould her, to develop her patience and her skill with her hands.

She remembered as well the times she had driven there with Ronnie, in the first flush of their romance, just two years previously during tropical evenings in the summer of 1961. They had embraced and pledged fidelity under the bright moonlight while the warm waves caressed the shore. Whenever she recalled those tender moments, time stood still and she longed for his gentle but passionate way with her.

'For all time,' he would pledge, 'till all the seas run dry, my dear,' quoting from their favourite Burns poem.

And she would respond, 'And the rocks melt with the sun.'

She sat in silence with the policemen, the Burns words running through her mind:

'And I will love thee still, my dear,

While the sands of life shall run.'

She hoped with all her fervour that he was safe.

10

They had met when the Royal Ballet Company was on a South African tour. Ronnie and his girlfriend had arrived from Johannesburg and were staying with Eleanor's next-door neighbour, Wendy Beckworth, a renowned artist. It was the Easter of 1960 and the Sharpeville massacre had taken place a short time before, on 21 March.

Eleanor knocked on Wendy's door to invite her to the ballet that evening. She had two tickets but her husband was refusing to go. It was *Swan Lake*. Wendy jumped at the chance.

When Ronnie playfully remarked, 'Nero fiddled while Rome burned,' Wendy replied instantly, 'Oh Ronnie, Eleanor and I are just innocent plebs.'

Eleanor later asked Wendy whether he really was critical of their attending the performance. Good God no, Wendy replied, he was just being playful. In fact she had taken them to a wild party for the Royal Ballet dancers at a friend's home. He and his girlfriend were as fun-loving as the rest. She had known them for a couple of years, as part of the Hillbrow bohemian set. But, she confided, he had a bee in his bonnet over this Sharpeville thing. 'You know, communist talk. He is bound to get over it.' Then she told Eleanor he had remarked that she was 'very pretty'. Eleanor blushed.

She saw him a few days later. Durban did indeed seem to be

on the point of burning. The newspapers had been full of the news of the government's declaration of a state of emergency and the round-up of hundreds of ANC leaders. The Africans of Cato Manor had embarked on a protest march to Durban Central Prison and were pouring through the Berea. One section of marchers had been stopped by the police on the very corner of the apartment block where Eleanor and Wendy lived.

Eleanor was in a state of agitation because her daughter was at a nursery school down the road. She had phoned her husband at work and he had instructed her to take his revolver and go and fetch their daughter at once. Ronnie was out on the street watching the drama unfold. She sought his advice. Leave your gun at home, he told her. The marchers were peaceful and orderly and any sight of the weapon could be dangerous for her. The safest place for her daughter would be to stay put at school.

She was grateful for the advice, which struck her as so much more sober than the hysterical chatter prevalent in white circles. She acted accordingly, and in fact the crowd of Africans, bedraggled but brave, had slowly turned back. She heard later how her art teacher, Harold Strachan, and his wife Maggy had stood facing the armed ranks of police – with guns ready to fire – in front of hundreds of marchers who had got through to the Central Prison where most detainees were being kept. They had undoubtedly helped prevent a further massacre.

Eleanor was a member of the tiny Liberal Party but found them rather irrelevant in the face of what was taking place. She knew Harold Strachan was close to the ANC and admired his and Maggy's courageous action in defiance of apartheid.

It was another year before she set eyes on Ronnie again at the Durban Film Club, which showed the kind of *avant-garde* films unavailable on the commercial circuit. He clearly was paying attention to her, for they exchanged flirtatious glances. She soon found him frequenting Griggs Bookshop but thought nothing unusual in this. He was clearly keen on purchasing good books. On one occasion, spotting him in the store, she told him that Solzhenitsyn's *One Day in the Life of Ivan Denisovich* was available and he promptly bought a copy, which he later came in to discuss with her.

Yes, he argued, it exposed Stalin's brutality as she had said when he purchased the copy, but why was the author being lauded in the West? Because he was a great writer, she responded. He conceded this but maintained it was largely because he undermined Soviet rule, which he defined as worker and peasant power, rather than the power of the capitalist class, which he referred to as the bourgeoisie. They agreed to continue the debate over coffee, and for a time she felt he was too earnest, too propagandistic for her liking. But nevertheless she could feel a tingling attraction building up inside her, uncertain whether it denoted a response to charm or challenge.

She soon found that he would ignore the other assistants and buy his books only from her. He had learnt of her separation from her husband and explained that he had taken a job with a Durban advertising agency as a film writer and had parted company with his girlfriend after the briefest of marriages. When she remarked that she found his class politics and his work in advertising a contradiction, he countered by saying everyone had to earn a living, as long as it was not robbing the poor. She argued that advertising was a form of deception and was surprised when he conceded that it was just that. Anyway, virtually every white person's income in South Africa was based on the exploitation of the black majority, he contended. He redeemed himself somewhat when he admitted that he had joined an advertising agency before his political consciousness was formed and was thinking of turning to something more principled. Like what? she asked. He was about to answer but shrugged his shoulders and joked, 'Maybe like robbing banks.'

They began to meet regularly for coffee or drinks after work. They went to the cinema one evening and afterwards she drove to the Blue Lagoon, where they were soon embracing. 'Come home with me,' she had suggested and, without waiting for his answer, deftly engaged the car's gears and drove up the hill at high speed to her Berea apartment. The maid, who was baby-sitting Brigid, withdrew to her quarters. After checking that her daughter was fast asleep, she led him to a divan in her sitting room, where they melted into one another's arms and made love for the first time.

They saw more and more of each other. He would call and they would go on picnics or drive to the beach and take Brigid along with them. It pleased her that he was so good with the young child, who clearly liked him.

Inevitably she was drawn into his political life. He would attend her friends' parties, where liberal intellectuals and university students met. They were care-free occasions which they thoroughly enjoyed. There would inevitably be discussions about the political situation in the country, and she noted how serious he would then become. Her liberal friends felt that he was far too radical, but she was attracted by the force of his arguments, which were scathing about the Liberal Party's opposition to a full universal franchise and their obvious fear of the ANC's closeness to the communists.

'This is both a race and a class struggle,' he explained to her, 'and the communists have understood the interrelationship of the two. Which is why they work so well with the ANC. They support mass action and have gone to prison with ANC members, earning their respect. The liberals think only of ending the colour bar and even then are too timid to call for full equality. They certainly oppose militant methods of struggle. So for them it is all talk and no action. Above all, they do not want to see a change in the economic order.'

At the parties he took her to, the majority of those present were Africans and Asians. Interacting with what were then termed 'non-whites' was not new to her. Her parents' circle, when she was growing up, had included a few very wealthy Indian and Chinese families, though certainly not the black students and workers she now associated with. Black and white danced and drank with fervour, belting out freedom songs. Everyone present appeared to be supporters of the ANC and critically debated the merits of liberalism, socialism, communism, passive resistance and violent struggle. Passive or non-violent resistance had been attempted for years but had always been put down by the government with force. The true terrorist was the apartheid state which, despite superficial differences between English and Afrikaner money, defended the interests of capital. A time came for any oppressed people when armed action was the only recourse.

One of the African students enjoyed goading liberal white

students with the statement 'Those who make peaceful change impossible make violent change inevitable'. He would challenge them with the demand: 'OK, who said that?' Responses generally were Mao Tsetung, Fidel Castro or Lenin. 'No,' he would crow delightedly, 'United States President John F. Kennedy.'

She found it natural and easy to get along with them, despite some of the harsher, propagandistic statements they made. There were times when they were invited to people's homes for the day and she was delighted at how naturally her daughter played with African and Indian children, oblivious of skin colour.

On occasion she and Ronnie would catch the bus home. At weekends there was no bus service for 'non-whites', who normally travelled in their own segregated buses. They were then permitted to occupy a few rows of seats at the very back of the bus for 'whites only'. The driver would allow just a few black people on at a time. The whites would choose seats as far to the front as possible so as to keep as much space as they could between themselves and the black passengers to the rear. This would infuriate her and Ronnie. Consequently when they got on they would stride past the white passengers, past the gap in the middle, and sit as close to the black passengers at the back, to show them that at least some whites did not believe they carried the plague. The whites who noticed would turn their heads and scowl. On one occasion, as they were alighting, one of the white passengers in the front turned to her companion and loudly hissed, 'Kaffirboeties!' In the most lady-like way Eleanor said to her, 'You have Africans in your house cooking your food, making your bed, looking after your children. Yet you will not sit near them on a bus. How strange!'

They had some fun writing letters to the press about Durban's bus service and its unwritten rules, pointing out the madness of apartheid and the racist system in the country. 'Where should your nanny and child sit,' they enquired of the white readership; 'closer to the whites or closer to the blacks?'

Ronnie asked her about the possibility of ordering books directly from abroad. That's what we do all the time, she told him. Yes, but what about a book that's banned or likely to be banned?

He explained that there was a book about guerrilla warfare by Che Guevara that had just been published in America. She checked the banned list. Since it was not yet listed, it meant that it had not yet come to the notice of the censor and she could add it to the bookshop's overseas orders. A form would need to be submitted to the censors but she could arrange to delay it until after the book had arrived. He would have to buy it the moment it came in.

'Can you get me twenty copies?' he asked.

She laughed. 'You do things in a big way.' Without fussing or prevaricating, she told him it would be arranged. When the books arrived, she cleared it through customs and arranged for him to come in and collect his order. No one in the shop was any the wiser.

11

'The trouble with this spot', she heard Malan say, 'is that the *blerrie coolies* think they own it. When is the government going to make this a no-go area for them?'

The two security policemen were monitoring the occupants of the cars parked along the sea front and at the river mouth by the Blue Lagoon. Most vehicles appeared to contain couples watching the fishermen on the rocks above the raging surf. 'I tell you,' Malan muttered to his companion, 'we got wind that the Jewboy was going to meet someone here tonight. *Gaan kyk.*' The other man got out to scout around and disappeared in the dark.

To her surprise Malan removed a flask from his pocket and took a huge gulp of what smelt like alcohol. 'Would you like some, lady?' She ignored him. He got out of the front seat and squeezed into the back of the Volkswagen to sit next to her. She was petrified and moved as far away as possible in the cramped space. 'Listen, lady, relax a bit. Grobler's given you a hard time. We're not all that mean – just doing a job, doing what we have to do for our country, following orders. This is time off for all of us, even you. I mean it, relax *net 'n bietjie.*' He took another gulp. 'I can take you out like this every night if you're good,' he said in a husky voice. She felt his hand on her knee and brushed it aside with distaste.

'Don't you dare try anything stupid!' she hissed at him. He pinched her thigh hard, very hard, but she bit her lip and struck out at him in fury. He spilt the liquor all over himself. He was raising his fist to strike her when his partner returned.

'Hell man, are you crazy? Cut it out. That couple in the other car are watching. Let's go.'

Back at the prison, the hard-faced wardress was not pleased that the Special Branch thought they could do as they wished in her domain. She resented their intrusion into the prison routine. To add to it, Malan was reeking of alcohol and the Afrikaner Calvinist in her disapproved of him bringing the young girl back so late. And that girl was feisty alright, she observed. Looks could deceive, she thought. For a girl who appeared so frail and weak like an undernourished model in a fashion magazine, she had great strength of mind.

'He molested me,' Eleanor shouted immediately they returned to the prison. 'He's just like Grobler. He's aping that dirty degenerate.'

Malan laughed. 'Stop fantasising, will you?'

Like Grobler, he was cock-sure of himself. It was her word against his, and his partner would always back him up.

As he left, Eleanor heard the wardress tell him, 'Officer, I am just asking that you comply with prison procedures.' She knew she was gaining ground, bit by bit.

Back in the cell the wardress encouraged her to eat her dinner. They had made an appetising meal of soup, chicken and mashed potato, with custard for dessert to tempt her. 'You've eaten nothing for two days now. You are going to get very ill. Come on now.'

Eleanor was getting to like the woman. Too bad, though;

she had a plan to follow. As she bore down on the tray of food, the wardress realised what was about to happen and pleaded, 'No, stop!'

Eleanor kicked the tray over and began screaming hysterically. 'Those swine keep assaulting me. Tonight they took me to the Blue Lagoon where he propositioned me and pinched me. I want him charged. I will not eat. I don't recognise their right to detain me. Just look at this bruise.' She lifted her dress and the wardress could see the angry red mark on her thigh.

Another wardress rushed in and they held her down on the bed until she grew quiet and stopped kicking and screaming. It was only after they left that she staggered to the basin to bathe her face and take a long drink.

12

The days of interrogation at Wentworth went by. Though the place remained a charnel house of brutality, the Special Branch made absolutely no headway with her. She turned on the tears and was able to weep effortlessly. She did so quietly, allowing her body to tremble as though with cold and she took to mumbling, 'This is unjust, this is unjust.'

They were clearly disconcerted: large men, awkward around women, nervous with the responsibility of dealing with a frail, stubborn, crazy white girl on a hunger strike who might die on their shift. Even Grobler appeared to lose steam and ideas, bored with her, and more often than not was engaged in interrogating others. When he came in sometimes, she spotted blood on his shirt and there was always the smell of alcohol on his breath.

On one occasion when they arrived at Wentworth there was no vacant office, so they left her in the reception area and went to sort things out. Another detainee was slumped in a chair, much the worse for wear. His eyes were bruised and badly swollen and his hands and legs were in chains. Eleanor recognised him as a factory worker, Shadrack Mapumulo, who worked closely with Curnick Ndlovu and Billy Nair.

'Shadrack, is that you?' she whispered. He stirred and looked quizzically at her.

'Eleanor, you here? Shame, sorry, sorry ... *amabuna inja.*'

'How are you, Shadrack?' she enquired softly and tenderly.

'It's bad. They use machine with handle, electric shocks on toes, fingers, even private parts ...' His body shuddered. 'Be careful. Bruno has sold us out.'

He struggled with the pain but was determined to continue: 'Bruno has tricked us. He's no good, never been genuine. He's been in prison many times before joining the Movement, for robbery. He's just an SB dog.'

She just managed a quick 'Courage, comrade' when one of Grobler's minions lumbered through and whisked her off for yet another day's interrogation. Her mind was on Shadrack, one of the older trade unionists. He was a thoughtful, mature person who would not accuse another comrade without evidence. If he was right – that Bruno Mtolo had been a common criminal, a thief who had served time without it coming to the notice of someone like Billy Nair – this would explain his skills. Maybe he had been an SB plant all along? Her mind turned to Shadrack Mapumulo. She was appalled at the poor man's suffering and the ordeal he and the others were going through. Their torture was so much worse than what she had to endure. It strengthened her resolve not to submit.

She was growing weaker and dizzier from not eating, but after the first two days found that the craving for food had become dulled. Every morning and every evening the tray of food, placed safely on a table outside her cell, went untouched.

Then after four or five days they brought the prison doctor to examine her. A hard-faced, elderly man, he was stiff and brusque but hesitant, too, and blamed her for becoming ill because she was not eating. She responded by saying she was

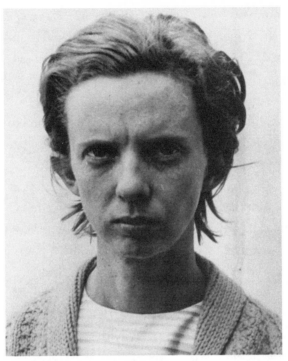

Photo of Eleanor taken during her detention, found in police files.

ill because the police, especially Grobler, had maltreated her. She told the doctor that she could not sleep and feared she was losing her mind because she was deeply worried about her small daughter. When he prescribed aspirin and sleeping tablets, she said she was not prepared to swallow any medicine given her in prison because she believed they would drug her to make her speak. In fact it was possible they were planning to poison her. He shook his head in disbelief, telling her she was being paranoid.

Though she could not tell what effect her assertions had on him, she hoped she was getting her message across.

13

The next day Grobler did not arrive at the usual time to fetch her for interrogation. This both pleased and worried her as she lay fully clothed on her bunk, hands behind her head, staring for the whole morning at the ceiling.

She did not regret becoming involved in the 'freedom struggle'. Once she had come in touch with the ANC, it seemed the most natural thing to do. While her relationship with Ronnie was the catalyst, her attraction to him only made it easier to come into contact with fellow South Africans whose whole life was dedicated to changing the racist injustice that she found she could no longer continue to ignore. When she met him she had been considering going with Brigid to Israel to live on a kibbutz. The egalitarian lifestyle that some of her Jewish friends spoke about appealed to her.

She was surprised at the vigorous way in which Ronnie disabused her of the idea, arguing that Israel had stolen the land from the Palestinian Arabs and was a colonial settlement supported and financed by the United States. It was no better than apartheid South Africa. She began to see the other side of the picture more clearly once she started attending discussion meetings at which various topics, South African and international, would feature. The lecturers were impressive veterans of the struggle such as Rowley Arenstein, a communist lawyer, and the two most senior trade unionists in Durban, Billy Nair and Stephen Dlamini. They would gather in someone's home, a dozen or so of them, young blacks and whites eager to learn. She soon began to introduce her own friends to these discussion circles, architectural students like John Bizzell and co-workers at Griggs. Soon they were joining Ronnie, Ebrahim Ismail Ebrahim and Sonny Singh in the distribution of ANC leaflets and painting slogans in the dead of night on walls around the city. This was exciting work and their numbers grew. Among Ronnie's circle was a woman called Thelma Nel, also from Johannesburg, with a tearaway temperament like his, which Eleanor associated with the jauntiness of that brash city. 'And I always thought of you as a bit of a weed,' she confessed to Eleanor on one of their painting sprees.

'A bit of a weed? Huh!' Ronnie shrugged his shoulders when Eleanor laughingly told him about the comment.

'Good,' he said, 'let people think you're inconsequential: that'll fool the Special Branch.'

She had started by organising fellow workers for the trade union, under the mentorship of Billy Nair, and had proved impressive, for the working-class white women were responsive to her easy manner and convincing motivation. She was careful to restrict the discussion initially to their conditions of employment, which were none too impressive though much better than the lot of black workers. Issues of pay, holiday allowance and pension schemes were the central topics. Billy advised her to wait for the right moment to introduce politics.

By then, however, she had begun to support Ronnie in a daring and dangerous new phase of the liberation struggle, which required brave and dedicated cadres of the Movement: weeds that would strangle the oxygen supply that kept the apartheid system alive. After years of non-violent struggle, the time for a change in methods had arrived. In response to the Sharpeville shootings and the outlawing of the ANC, and the continuing use of state violence to break strikes and peaceful protests, the Mandela leadership had decided to embark on the first phase of an armed struggle: a sabotage campaign to be waged by the newly created military wing, Umkhonto weSizwe (Spear of the Nation), known by its members as MK.

Eleanor became one of MK's earliest recruits and one of its first women operatives. This was done with Billy Nair's agreement, for he had become intimately involved as one of MK's initial leaders. The slow work of trade unionism would have to take a back seat for a while. When Rowley Arenstein, with whom they played chess, talked politics and discussed films, argued fiercely against the new form of struggle, he could only guess at their involvement.

Eleanor was invited to a hush-hush meeting along with a handful of promising junior activists. While she was there, an imposing bearded man with a grave expression was ushered in. To the manifest drawing-in of collective breath, he was recognised as Nelson Mandela. Having disappeared the year before to lead the clandestine struggle, the 'Black Pimpernel', as he became known, had recently slipped back into the country after a visit abroad. He spoke quietly about the wave of independence struggles in Africa and the need to step up resistance at home. Within a week he was captured at a roadblock on the Durban–Johannesburg highway. He had met with far too many groups in Durban, and elsewhere, and it was clear he had been betrayed. The Natal command of MK, smarting under the stigma of Mandela's arrest on their turf, resolved to intensify the bombing campaign. Eleanor, as devastated as everyone else, was grateful for the opportunity to act.

Riding pillion on Ronnie's motorbike, they reconnoitred a site where a road construction company was storing its dynamite supply. The new road was being cut through nearby hills but there was little activity at the prefabricated storeroom, which was enclosed by a formidable barbed wire fence in the bush. Entrance was through an equally formidable gate. Bruno Mtolo, who had located the site, informed them that at night a watchman was on duty but regularly absented himself to retire to a nearby shebeen for a long bout of drinking. In fact Bruno had heard the watchman talking about his job at that very tavern, which was how the presence of the store had become known to him.

They laid out a blanket and picnic basket on the grass verge – a white couple on their travels. There were a few workers about who barely glanced at them. A truck arrived, the gate was unlocked and they watched as the vehicle drove in. Two men went into the storeroom and emerged carrying a few wooden boxes, which they loaded on to the truck.

Ronnie, talking it over with Eleanor, mused that wire-cutters would be required to get through the outer gate. The storeroom would have to be broken into. With nobody about, Eleanor sauntered over to the padlocked gate, had a cursory look, and returned to the picnic spot. 'Well,' she said to him, 'I've noted the brand name of the padlock and its serial number. It might be possible to buy one at a hardware store.'

'Fat chance,' he said. She kept silent.

For a few days she spent her lunch hours conscientiously checking padlocks available by the dozens in various hardware stores, searching for the particular brand and inspecting the serial numbers. Ronnie told her she was wasting her time. The leadership had already decided on the wire-cutting option. 'OK,' she said in her soft-spoken way. 'I'm getting close. I bet you a drink I'll succeed.'

A few days later they met at a favourite haunt. She was sitting at a table under a palm tree, looking cool and demure. As he joined her she handed him a key and said, 'Make mine a gin and tonic.'

Later he told her how well the raid had worked. The night-watchman, as anticipated, was nowhere in sight. They had taken heavy wire-cutters along, doubting that the key would do the trick. When he inserted it in the lock, it had worked like a charm.

The newspapers told her the rest of the story, declaring with banner headlines: 'Dynamite Stolen from Pinetown Company.' Almost half a ton of dynamite had disappeared after thieves broke into a road construction store in the bush. The police were investigating.

One thing led to another. She had earned her spurs. Now she would drive the get-away car for Ronnie's unit on a daring mission. It was to be MK's most ambitious operation in Natal and possibly the entire country. For weeks she helped him plot the province's electricity grid system. They rode around on his motorbike tracking the electricity pylons linking power station to power station. When the pylons veered off from alongside the major roads to cross the countryside, cut through the sea of green sugarcane or surmounted the rolling hills, they used side roads or even pathways well off the beaten track, to follow the route the electricity was directed along. It was an achievement they were justly proud of when they had mapped the complete circuit, showing the electricity supply lines linking Natal's major towns, industrial areas and coastal hamlets. Once they had come to know the terrain intimately, it proved easy to target three points – three huge pylons – hundreds of kilometres apart, which if correctly dynamited would disrupt the power supply of the entire province.

She realised there would be three units operating independently and using timing devices to ensure that the selected pylons would be simultaneously destroyed. She drove Ronnie, David Ndawonde and Justice Mpanza – both ANC activists and MK cadres from KwaMashu township – to their allocated pylons not far from the province's biggest coal-driven power station outside Pinetown, off the main road between Durban and Pietermaritzburg. They carried with them a bag with the dynamite sticks, fuses, detonators and timing devices.

It was a dark night with no moon. Once she dropped them off, she had to park the car in deep shadow, waiting tensely for the three of them to return after placing the charges. Thirty minutes' waiting was a long time in such circumstances. She hoped that everything would go smoothly, that they would not be disturbed, that there would be no passing pedestrian or vehicle to bother them. Far off in the distance she could hear motor cars whining up the hill to Pietermaritzburg, and nearer afield a lone dog howling outside a peasant homestead, and then, further away, the answering barks of neighbouring hounds. The rhythmical humming of the cicadas was comforting in the bush.

The night was so dark that she only saw them when they arrived back at the car. They had completed the task and she sensed they were elated. She drove off as quietly as possible, headlights extinguished, coaxing the vehicle along the dirt track until they came to a point where she could drive on to the main road. She flicked the lights on and drove steadily back to the city. They had ninety minutes in which to drop the two comrades close to KwaMashu, park the vehicle at a safe garage and get back to their cottage on the Berea before the dynamite would be detonated.

They were back in the house with twenty minutes to spare. They sat in the small sitting room, starting a game of chess, anxiously counting down the time. Suddenly the cottage was plunged into darkness. 'Christ, we've done it,' he whispered triumphantly, embracing her. They rushed outside to assess the extent of the power failure. The entire street was in darkness, not a home or building in light. They walked, almost ran, up the hill to the park at the top of their road with its panoramic view of Durban. The darkness was dense and all-pervading. The busy city centre, normally bright with its lights glowing, was lost in the black void. They hugged each other and walked swiftly back to the cottage, knowing that before long the Special Branch would arrive to check if they were at home. Eleanor lit candles and they sat holding hands talking in soft tones. It was all going like a film script, for as expected they heard the Volkswagen coming to a halt outside. A knock on the door and Eleanor answered. It was one of the SB officers who had come to see if they were in. Had they been at home all evening?

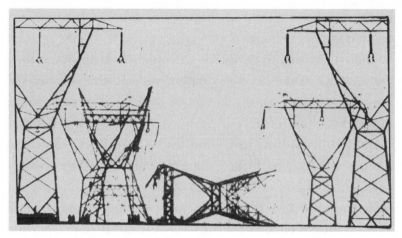

A newspaper photo of electricity pylons toppled by explosions.

'Oh yes, although we took a short walk earlier. What's going on?'

'You'll read about it in tomorrow's paper.'

In the event the daily paper was greatly delayed. The headlines were sensational. Three pylons had been felled by dynamite, to the north, south and west of Durban, disrupting power supply to the city, to Pietermaritzburg and all the coastal towns. It was clear that the dynamite stolen from Pinetown a few months earlier had been used and that the saboteurs were becoming more professional and daring. The police were investigating.

By contrast, she reflected, their second big mission, the bombing of the Durban Central Post Office and the SB office, was far simpler if more dangerous. Were she to be linked to them, she could land in very hot water indeed. She fretted over the possibility that the police might come up with clues but thought it unlikely, unless they produced eyewitnesses.

She was relieved that Bruno Mtolo knew nothing of her involvement in these bombings.

It had been a humid evening in Durban shortly before Christmas 1962. The city was full of holiday-makers from up-country. The city centre, with its statue of Queen Victoria, imposing colonial-style City Hall, General Post Office and impressively designed railway station, was a hive of activity – the white citizenry and visitors ostensibly without a care in the world. The MK leadership had considered this a good opportunity to get the message of resistance across to white South Africa and give them a rude awakening.

Eleanor and Ronnie would blend in perfectly. The bomb in her shopping bag consisted of a powerful explosive mixture within a cast-iron sealed pipe and a timing device. This was wrapped in brown paper to make it look like a parcel. They had been ultra careful to ensure there were no tell-tale fingerprints on the device. Eleanor used a public toilet off the square to set the timer, putting on skin-tight, plastic gloves. Ronnie waited for her to emerge and accompanied her across the street to the Post Office. They climbed the stairs together, he following a step behind to shield her. As cool as a cucumber she posted the package through the aperture and heard it rolling safely down the internal chute.

They were professional saboteurs by this stage and took a slow walk around the square. 'This we have to see,' he remarked. She was as keen as he was and they took a seat on a bench, holding hands, looking like the numerous other pedestrians taking the early evening air.

When the bomb exploded with a huge bang from within the building they involuntarily jumped. It was not designed to injure but to scare the living day-lights out of anyone within a kilometre radius. Clouds of dense smoke rose from the aperture. Muscular young men dashed to ascertain what had occurred and prove their manhood if possible. White faces everywhere wore shocked and frightened expressions. The city square emptied fast. The two bombers quietly left and made for a downtown cinema, which might provide some kind of alibi. The film was *Tunes of Glory* with Alec Guinness. They thought the title appropriate to the occasion.

The other mission, the attack on the SB office near the law courts, on the other hand nearly went terribly wrong. Firstly there had been someone in the dark approach lane behind the building who appeared to be observing them. That was when she and Ronnie had embraced, long and amorously, to allay the man's suspicion.

It was an old, two-storey wooden building, which they had checked out many times. The lower floor consisted of a few offices linked to the law courts. The upper floor housed offices of the traffic police, but they had noted that the SB used a rear office when attending court hearings. They had also observed that the building was generally shut at night. To their disappointment they now saw that the lights were on in one of the traffic police offices. Well, they reasoned, maybe the lights had been left on by mistake. Though Ronnie was ready to take a chance, she was nervous and unsure. He had ruled her out from entering the building anyway. It involved a difficult climb over a fence at the rear. Once he was over that obstacle she would hand him the explosive device through the fence and keep watch. He was soon creeping up the back stairs to the top floor and then disappeared from sight.

To her utter consternation she saw a few uniformed policemen entering the front of the building, switch on the lights and ascend the front steps. She whistled from the shadows, aware that he could not but have noticed their arrival, and just prayed that he would be able to stay out of sight. She hoped he would retreat in time and come scurrying down the rear stairs. There was no sign of him. The policemen were on the second floor. If they were going to the SB office, the game would be well and truly over for him. But with relief she noticed they had entered the office with the lights on. Probably because it was a usual humid Durban evening, they kept the door ajar.

Ronnie soon reappeared, moving silently and swiftly down the back stairs. He waited for her to signal the all-clear and slipped effortlessly over the fence. She could feel him trembling as they moved arm in arm as quickly as possible out of the area, ending up at a hotel where they had quite a few stiff shots of alcohol.

The next day the newspapers reported that an incendiary device had gone off at the building. Because there were police on the premises the fire was swiftly extinguished, causing only minor damage. What the MK command concluded, however, was that the mission had delivered a psychological blow to a prime enemy. That adversary would, of course, leave no stone unturned to punish the perpetrators. Pay-back time had arrived with the ninety-day detention laws – the aptly named Sabotage Act.

14

As she lay on her prison bunk, staring at the ceiling, waiting for Grobler to fetch her for interrogation, the questions kept nagging at her. How long could she withstand them? How long would these secrets be safe with her? Of course Bruno could tell them a great deal about the MK operations, but she had to hold out, particularly to defend the political leadership both in Durban and Johannesburg, for whom she had been a key secret link and underground courier. In fact she was a very secret agent whose role only Ronnie and a few leaders were aware of.

She thought of people like Stephen Dlamini, a gentlemanly, old-world trade union leader who loved classical music and worked with other political veterans like the vigorous M.P. Naicker and George and Vera Ponnen in the city. Vera was from London's East End, who had participated in anti-fascist street battles before the war, and had arrived in South Africa twenty years earlier to become a leading communist organiser. She had married an Indian trade unionist, George Ponnen, said to be the only man capable of keeping the garrulous Vera quiet. With Stephen Dlamini and Billy Nair, George had built a powerful labour movement in Natal. Eleanor was their most reliable link with what remained of the national leadership in Johannesburg. Funds and sensitive documents all flowed through her hands as their key courier.

She regretted knowing too much. At the Johannesburg end she reported to Bram Fischer, one of the country's leading left-wing advocates, and to Hilda Bernstein, a banned communist orator and writer, who appeared to be reorganising things following the Rivonia arrests on 11 July, the month before. They had clearly been assisting Goldreich and Wolpe, who made a sensational escape from police custody on 11 August, just eight days before her own detention. The situation was extraordinary and they were under great pressure. In fact they were responsible for Ronnie, who was hiding with a friend of hers in Johannesburg. As she lay on the bunk, the knowledge weighed heavily on her mind and she tried in vain to blot out these dangerous associations.

When things start going wrong, in an underground resistance movement as in any other organisation, efforts to limit the damage often fall on fewer shoulders. So it was that Eleanor was loaded with more and more responsibilities. Not for a moment did she shirk them. When Stephen Dlamini and the Ponnens ascertained that she was far too deeply implicated and in grave danger of being arrested, they sent her to Johannesburg with the recommendation that she and Ronnie be sent out of the country. Bram Fischer considered this at length. He discussed the situation with her but in the end felt that they needed her to stay put just a little while longer until they could find an adequate replacement. Without batting an eyelid she accepted his request, saw Ronnie all too briefly in Johannesburg, and returned to her battle station in Durban.

The bookstore became the front line. This was the last available link for those on the run to pass messages through her to the remaining Durban leadership and between them and Johannesburg. They followed the classic methods of clandestine contact. If Eleanor and the courier knew each other, the arrangement was simple and straightforward though always delicate in the timing and the rules of security. If the contact was delivering a document it was handed to her with a book for purchase. Similarly if she had a document that the courier was collecting, it would be hidden within the pages of a book already packaged and handed over as a purchase. If she held a red pen or had it clipped to her dress, the signal conveyed was 'keep away' – the time was either inconvenient or there was danger. 'Come back later.'

If Eleanor did not know the contact, then recognition signs and passwords were to be used. The contact, whether male or female, would carry a copy of *Time* magazine. They would know that at exactly noon, a fair-haired young woman assistant would be standing at the art section. They would need to ask her: 'Do you have Olive Schreiner's *Cry, the Beloved Country*?'

To which she would reply: 'That's by Alan Paton. Olive Schreiner wrote *Story of an African Farm*, my favourite South African novel.'

For Eleanor to be absolutely certain, the contact would have to add something like: 'Well, let me take both books.' And then the transfer of secret documents could take place.

More and more of such visitors were black people, who did not normally frequent an up-market bookstore like Griggs. Usually they were in need of funds. So Eleanor had to enlist the support of two fellow staff members to cover for her, especially when her mother, 'Old Eagle-eye' as they called her, hovered near. Sybilla Higgs, the tall young woman, and Jill Richburn, who was related to Alan Paton, would distract her or, for that matter, any other curious staff member.

Eleanor was well aware that if she broke and divulged information of this kind, the SB would find ways of using it to trap countless comrades. The responsibility frightened her.

What next? She was sure the police would be accumulating more and more information and clues to confront her with. And then, how would she behave if she was confronted by her parents being arrested, leaving the fate of Brigid to be determined by the SB. Would she really be able to hold out? The thought of surrender sent shivers down her spine.

15

At noon the wardress brought a placid-looking man to see her. He introduced himself as a psychiatrist and said the authorities were anxious about her and had called him in to examine her. After a medical examination in which he took her blood pressure and tested her reflexes, he asked her a series of routine-sounding questions. What was her name? What day of the week was it? Did she know where she was? She realised he was establishing whether she was compos mentis. When he asked if she knew why she was being detained, she let rip about the injustice of her arrest. For good measure she told him she was afraid of being overheard and he promptly arranged to interview her in private in the exercise yard.

He listened patiently to her whole story, including Grobler's behaviour, and held her hand while she wept, squeezing it sympathetically. He told her she was not in good shape, was dehydrated and in all probability had suffered from a nervous collapse. She needed rest and, above all, food and rehydration.

Things happened quickly after that. The psychiatrist returned in the afternoon with the prison commandant, a man in brown uniform with the rank of colonel, who frowned at her suspiciously. She was told she was being referred to a mental hospital for assessment. She was ill and must begin eating at once or she would die, he muttered in irritation. But her removal from prison was conditional on her eating. She readily agreed but would only do so once she was moved. Her father was allowed to see her for ten minutes; he brought her some fresh clothing. She was so used to seeing him as a dapper, urbane socialite, yet he could only weep uncontrollably when he saw her.

Before she left prison Grobler brought in a police photographer. Mug shots were taken of a frowning Eleanor, her features wan and drawn, her hair dishevelled, her eyes with dark circles. But her chin was up, her expression livid and defiant.

She was ushered out of the huge prison doors into Grobler's Volkswagen. 'Tell this man not to molest me,' was her parting plea to the prison commandant, who looked on in astonishment.

They drove in silence. Grobler and his partner were not in conversational mood, an air of defeat about them. They drove west of Durban on the main arterial road to Johannesburg. She began to worry as she had hoped she would be taken to a city hospital near her family and friends with a good possibility of escape.

It was an hour's drive to Pietermaritzburg. They drove past Pinetown where the dynamite had been stolen; past another point where she had taken Ronnie's group to dynamite the huge electricity pylon. On the misty hills at Kloof they passed near to her parents' property, a smallholding surrounded by a dense hedge with a few dilapidated outhouses which were hardly ever visited. It was here that she had secreted Ronnie within a week of his escape from their Durban cottage. He was then joined by some other comrades, including Bruno

Mtolo and Ebrahim Ismail Ebrahim, and they began to draw up plans to regroup after what had been a wave of devastating arrests. As she came to realise through the interrogation sessions, it was at Kloof that the police later arrested Bruno, after following a township contact who had gone there to meet him. Fortunately by then, Ronnie and Ebrahim had relocated further up the highway to a rented house at Hillcrest.

That weekend she had been to Johannesburg to report to Bram Fischer and receive money and instructions for those on the run. She always found his courteous presence reassuring. Despite having to deal with the matter of the Rivonia arrests, and as senior advocate prepare for the trial that would follow, he was conscientious and caring in his dealings with her. He clearly liked her and remarked affectionately that she was so like his younger daughter.

When she returned to Durban on the Sunday afternoon she had gone straight to see her own young daughter at her parents' home. They were in a perplexed state and told her the police had come to see them, because a 'native' had been arrested at their Kloof property the previous day. The police had obtained their address from the Kloof estate agent who had the property on his books. To the police they denied knowledge of the 'native' and at the same time withheld the fact that Eleanor had asked them just a couple of months previously whether a university biologist could camp out there as part of a field study, to which they had readily agreed.

'Who is this native?' her parents asked her, but she just dashed off, desperate to warn Ronnie in time. 'Speak to you later,' she told them.

Grobler's Volkswagen droned up the long drive through

Hillcrest. As they passed, she glanced along the ridge where Ronnie had rented the second house. It was there she had rushed to after receiving the disastrous news from her parents about the arrest at their Kloof property. The house was at the end of a dirt road and she began desperately knocking on the front door. Ronnie, pistol in hand, emerged with Ebrahim from the adjacent bush. They were extremely tense and relieved to see her. She gave them the news she had learnt from her parents. They explained that it must have been Bruno who had been arrested. He was staying with them and had gone to the Kloof property the previous day to meet a contact. When he did not return that Saturday evening as expected, they had debated whether to decamp or not, which is why she had found them hiding in the safety of the bush. They thought he might have been arrested but on the other hand there was the possibility that he had simply gone temporarily AWOL. Perhaps he had been to a shebeen and got drunk.

With her news, there was now no doubt about Bruno. They needed to clear out at once. She had arranged for a Pietermaritzburg comrade to come and fetch them. Having dropped them off at a point near the main road to await their pick-up, she sped off in a cloud of dust to attend to other pressing business in Durban.

Driving with Grobler, a subdued but hopeful Eleanor saw from the roadway signs that they were approaching the psychiatric institution called Fort Napier, which had been a British colonial garrison in the 19th century. Everyone knew of the place, the ostensibly sane never failing to joke about the 'loony bin' in Maritzburg. Since 1927 it had been catering for the mentally disturbed – from regular nervous break-downs to the hopelessly deranged. It was a forbidding-looking Victorian complex, with high walls, guarded security gates and rows of former barracks converted into hostels for the patients.

They halted at the main entrance. Though the huge, heavy gates were open to allow traffic to pass, they waited their turn to explain to a security guard what their business was. Grobler turned to talk to her for the first time that day. He was grinning: 'You think you're smart, missis. Just wait and see where we are going to put you. Your prison cell was like paradise compared to the lock-up here where they keep the psychos [pronounced *sick ou's*].'

16

The thought of the lock-up chilled her, and she watched intently as the security guard waved them through the outer gate. They drove through the spacious grounds, the manicured lawns, the well-trimmed shrubs, past row upon row of straight-lined, two-storey buildings.

She thought of the similarity between the prisons, the military camps, the asylums of the country – even the railway stations with their well-ordered gardens – which were all laid out in similar fashion. It was as if someone with a compulsive mental disorder had meticulously arranged the cans in a cupboard in exact straight lines. It imposed the notion of desired control and order.

The Volkswagen came to a halt at a grim-looking, single-storey, barrack-style building, with metal doors and barred windows with mesh screens. The metal bars were painted shiny white.

The outer door was made of heavy iron and had a small grate. A face appeared. When Grobler announced who they were, the door was slowly pushed open by a nurse in a white uniform who escorted them through a dim corridor with a row of single cells on one side. It was late afternoon and the cell doors were ajar. Eleanor saw some patients sitting listlessly within, one banging her head against a padded wall, another

71

staring zombie-like into space, and yet another lying open-eyed in bed talking to herself. A large dishevelled woman shuffled stiffly past, hands tearing at her hair, crying miserably: 'My baby, my baby has died. They killed my baby!' Large, burly nurses in starched white uniforms stood by, watching their charges intently.

As they navigated their way through the communal area, the buzz of excitement grew. Some patients, giggling hysterically, tried to touch Eleanor. As bedraggled as she felt she was, she must have seemed glamorous to them. The inmates wore faded grey smocks and looked old and drugged with medication. She recoiled in horror.

As she was led to the Head Matron's office, she was aware of many glazed eyes following her every move. The Matron was a tough old woman in a navy uniform, with a watch and military ribbons pinned to her tunic, who spoke in a cultivated Natal accent, like a cheerful teacher at a boarding school. She told Eleanor in a chummy way not to be afraid of the patients: 'They are a harmless lot – actually very friendly. Not to worry. You will be placed in your own cell. Most of the inmates are accommodated in a common ward. Just a few, shall I say "unique", cases are confined to cells.'

'Now,' she looked deep into Eleanor's eyes, 'the arrangement that brings you here is that you start eating this evening. I am aware you've taken nothing for six days, so you will be given some soda water and dry biscuits right away, followed by a substantial meal in an hour. Your assessment will commence tomorrow. The Medical Superintendent of Fort Napier and a doctor will see you then. In the meantime, please co-operate with us. You must obey our rules.'

Grobler watched Eleanor with cold, dead eyes. 'Yes!' she agreed with alacrity, 'anything, Matron, anything to get away from this evil man.'

Grobler knew that the Matron would interpret Eleanor's remark as typical of paranoia. 'Oh, stop being silly, missis, you and your persecution complex.' He shook his head as though concerned about her state of mind and could not resist a parting shot as he turned to leave: '*Moenie* worry *nie*, we will be back for you.'

She ate a hearty meal in her cell. It was typical institution food: watery noodle soup, runny mince and peas, a treacle pudding and a glass of milk. She tucked in.

There were faces peering through the bars within the cell door, the faces of her fellow inmates: grotesque, pitiful and (she hated to use the word) zombie-like in appearance. Some thrust their hands through the bars to reach for her. God, she thought, will I ever get used to them? She was relieved when a bell sounded and she heard the women being herded like sheep to their beds. It was soon lights out. But there were disturbing new sounds to get used to: wailing and sobbing interspersed with shrieks and insane laughter that persisted on and off through the night. She also heard the weeping woman crying, 'They have killed my baby, they have nailed him to the Cross. Sweet Jesus, gentle Jesus.' She thought of her own child but felt strong and resolved to escape and somehow be reunited with Ronnie and her daughter.

Whatever fears she might have of Fort Napier, she was convinced it offered a way out. As mentally disturbed as these inmates were, they were nowhere near as mad as Grobler and most of the Special Branch – a gang of sadistic brutes and torturers in the service of an insane government. Better to be among these poor wretches than in the hands of those psychopaths outside. Round one to me, she thought; now for round two. She fell into a deep sleep for the first time since her arrest.

17

Next morning Eleanor had to be coaxed out of her cell. She was petrified of having to mix with the inmates. Lying in her iron bed on a threadbare mattress, she listened to the sounds of their awakening as the thin light of dawn seeped into her strange new world. The mentally deranged were slow to awake, but like drunkards shaking off the after-effects of a night's binge, their groans intensified as they became reacquainted with their inner demons.

A nurse came to her cell just before 6 am and unlocked the door. She was shaking her head. 'It's a blue Monday. Last night's dosage must have been too strong. Come, I'll show you where you can wash. Breakfast's at six fifteen.'

Anticipating Eleanor's reluctance to leave the safety of her cell, she said briskly, 'The sooner you get used to our little community the better.'

'But they wouldn't leave me alone last night.'

'You're a new girl, that's all. In no time they'll take you for granted. Just relax and act natural.'

Act natural, in a place like this? Eleanor sniggered to herself and realised she must be on the mend. Anything better than Grobler and the Special Branch.

After her first hot shower in a week, she looked and felt a

great deal better. The Matron had given her shampoo and her fair hair had regained its lustre.

The nurse led her through to the dining room where the inmates were crowded around long refectory tables and ate with plastic spoons. Quite a few were being fed by nursing staff. Some of the others, called the 'dribblers', made a game attempt at putting spoon to mouth but much of the food simply dribbled down their chins. Then there were the 'droolers', who sat with heads slumped, looking blankly into their plates, saliva running from the corner of their mouths while waiting for assistance.

The nurse placed her at a table set aside from the rest. 'This is for patients who can feed themselves,' she explained.

There was a group of four middle-aged women already seated. At first she thought they must be staff members, clerks from administration, because they did not look deranged and wore presentable dresses rather than grey smocks. They also used plastic knives and forks.

As she tentatively sat down at the table, they nodded at her. Eleanor was reserved when meeting strangers and ventured a polite 'Good morning' as she helped herself to a bowl of porridge.

'Well, well, so you're the new girl who's causing such a stir,' was the well-spoken manner in which one of them addressed her. She continued by way of explanation: 'My dear, we're the sane bunch here – if you can call alcoholics sane.' The others sniggered. 'Our families have signed us in, bless them, to try and force us to dry out.'

'Families?' one of the others snorted. 'They're just bloody ashamed of us. Out of sight, out of mind.'

The first woman smiled and held out her hand. 'I'm Swanepoel – "Swanny" to my friends.'

Eleanor shook hands. 'I'm Eleanor. Pleased to meet you.'

At the back of her mind she thought that perhaps the woman was a Special Branch plant. All of them struck her as coming from working-class backgrounds with the hardened expressions of serious drinkers. But as introductions were made around the table, she saw in them some friendly company and a shield, if necessary, from the mentally disturbed inmates. She would in any case maintain her vigilance and keep an appropriate distance. All four were naturally curious about her as she was of them, but breakfast did not last longer than thirty minutes, so the initial conversation, in between the porridge, sweet black tea and thickly cut bread and jam, did not go much further than initial introductions and a short chat about the inmates. They reiterated what the nurse had told Eleanor about the patients generally being quite docile.

Swanny explained that the only treatment provided was heavy sedation in the morning and evening, and sometimes at noon, which kept the hyperactivity under control and the inmates safely doped 'out of their skulls in a chemical straitjacket', as she put it. When they were over-sedated, as apparently had happened the night before, the scene the following day could be chaotic, as she had observed.

Some patients had been there for twenty years or more. If they had ever had any family, they had long been abandoned. Some were murderesses, like old Hetty, the one who went on endlessly about baby Jesus. 'She strangled her infant son at birth over twenty years ago. But that's because her own father had impregnated her and she killed him too. Doused his bed with petrol while he slept off the effects of booze and sleeping tablets she had ground into the liquor. She stabbed him a hundred times with a pair of scissors and set the bed alight. They say it took him weeks to die. Good riddance. He deserved it.'

'As for me,' said Swanny, 'General Smuts was my lover, and when he dumped me I hit the bottle big time.'

The others all laughed and Eleanor giggled with them. 'You don't say? General Smuts, the former Prime Minister? Is that right?'

'Yes,' said Francina, another of the quartet, 'and I drank myself into the ground when Errol Flynn dumped me on the scrap heap.'

'Just kidding,' said Swanny, 'although you can bet there were some male bastards involved in our fall from grace, for sure. Damn their pig eyes,' and there was a note of raw bitterness in her voice.

As breakfast ended and Eleanor had to prepare for the meeting with the Superintendent, she explained that she was in trouble with the police, who were hunting for her lover. 'Well, I hope he's worthy of you,' muttered Francina.

Swanny, who had taken an instant liking to Eleanor, asked if she played rummy.

'Do I play rummy?' she responded, her large blue-grey eyes lighting up for the first time since her arrest. 'You mean you play rummy here?'

'Best card sharps in Fort Napier,' Swanny retorted. 'Care to join the school, dear heart?' The term of endearment was her way of declaring an affinity.

'If they allow me, you can bet on it,' she answered. 'I'm off

78

to my assessment now. What should I know about it?'

'Be obedient. Don't rock the boat. But don't swallow their medication, unless you want to be a walking zombie like the poor wretches here. Before long you'll be dribbling. We've seen it. Mark my words.'

18

The man in charge of Fort Napier had the Orwellian title of Physician Superintendent. He arose from behind a magnificent oak desk, in his white coat, a portrait of the country's Prime Minister, Dr Verwoerd, smiling benignly like one of his patients on the wall behind him, and peered at her with some curiosity. This was the man referred to as the 'Super'. She knew that his signature on a document could alter a person's life for all time.

Eleanor was delighted to find the psychiatrist from Durban present. He, too, was now dressed in the regulation white coat associated with his profession. She had prepared herself for the interview by subduing her new-found surge of spirits and contrived to look strained, dejected and tearful.

The Super turned to his associate. 'This is Dr —,' he said in almost a hushed voice, 'one of our senior psychiatrists. He has referred you here for assessment. His professional opinion is that you have suffered a nervous collapse like many of our patients in the open section of Fort Napier. You must understand that you are still legally under police arrest and for that reason they have insisted that you be kept under confinement in our small prison while you are on referral here. Because you are a detainee and not serving a sentence, you are permitted to wear civilian clothing. While here, you are our responsibility and I must request that you comply with our rules and not try to escape. I am pleased that you have started eating. The doctor will be handling your case and will be taking you to his consulting room right away,' he concluded.

The psychiatrist greeted her with a pleasant smile and enquired about her condition, and how she was finding the institution. He, too, remarked that he was pleased she was eating.

Eleanor said she was happy to be with them because the Durban Special Branch had been so vicious with her. Lieutenant Grobler in particular had gone out of his way to persecute her. He had physically assaulted her and was disgustingly filthy-minded because of his hatred for her boyfriend. In her opinion he was a psychopath. With that she began sobbing quietly.

'Please don't let them come anywhere near me,' she pleaded. 'Those evil men are out to get me.' She knew the thought of 'paranoia' would come to their minds. But who in the insanity of apartheid South Africa, she thought, could be totally free of paranoia? She was able to play that card to perfection. The psychiatrist assured her she was safe at Fort Napier.

She accompanied him to his office and sat alone with him for an hour. He checked her blood pressure and general physical condition and said she needed a lot of rest and wanted her to take some medication to ease the tension. He needed to bring her blood pressure down, which was dangerously high. When she insisted that she would have none of the drugs that the general patients clearly lived on, he assured her that she would be given a much milder sedative, 'which is what half the middle class women of Durban swear by'. He shrugged his shoulders in a resigned way about the treatment of her fellow inmates. She needed to realise that there were huge staff shortages and lack of resources and that to reform the system needed a huge mind-shift. 'You probably know better than me that the state sector is in no mood for progressive change. Their focus is on security. The private sector, where the well-off can afford quality service, is another matter entirely. I'm an optimist and that's where change will come.' If only more whites felt like him, she thought, things could get better.

He asked her a few routine questions as he had the previous day and then proceeded with a few straightforward psychology tests, starting with responses to words. She did not have to make up the violent associations that came to mind, so when he prompted her with 'man' she replied 'wild' instead of 'woman', which would have been her normal choice. Similarly, to 'red' she responded 'blood' rather than 'flag' and to 'green' she replied 'sick' instead of 'grass'. With the Rorschach blot test she imagined all manner of brooding threats, such as prowling beasts, swooping raptors and twisted breasts.

After a while she wondered whether she was fooling the psychiatrist or not. Though her common sense told her that psychiatry must be wise to the endless wiles of patients and that the test would take into account attempts at deception, she let her instincts guide her. He sat expressionless before her, placidly observing her every expression. Somehow she sensed he had empathy with her.

His office had a good if distant view of the main gate. Eleanor could hardly believe her luck because if she was to succeed in an escape attempt it was vital that she should know how security operated there. As he was seated with his back to

82

the window, she focused on him in such a way that she could follow movement in the distance without difficulty. As on her arrival the afternoon before, the gates were kept open, possibly being locked only after dark. Security guards stopped vehicles and talked to the drivers; some showed papers before being allowed to proceed. The interiors of vans and occasionally the boots of cars were inspected, presumably to counter theft. What Eleanor found interesting was that most pedestrians appeared to walk freely in and out: the guards gave them no more than a cursory glance. Perhaps only one in ten was stopped, a question or two seemed to be asked, a document produced.

As she was escorted back to the lock-up, she had the chance to take in more of the surroundings. Nurses in starched white uniforms walked briskly between buildings. Other administrative staff in ordinary dress did likewise. Traffic and pedestrians flowed in and out of the vast grounds. Some patients in the upper floors of the hostels gazed listlessly from their windows. Others dressed in gowns, in some cases accompanied by nurses, walked slowly around the grounds, a few shuffling stiffly, while others seemingly talked to themselves. One or two were busy tending the flower beds or weeding the grass. There was an air of order and calm about the asylum.

Once again it occurred to her that the Wentworth House of Truth, as Grobler called it, was where the real maniacs were running riot. That was where the psychopaths ruled. There and in Pretoria, the seat of government, she thought bitterly, and in Cape Town where the all-white parliament rubber-stamped the legislation like zombies. She was reminded of a

Roy Campbell poem of the 1930s: 'A wondrous land South Africa/ Where pumpkins into parliament go/ And cabbages into professors grow.' The most sane and rational people, like Nelson Mandela, Walter Sisulu, Govan Mbeki, Billy Nair and Helen Joseph, were thrown into jail or placed under house arrest; and white society brayed approval like donkeys.

Resting in her cell, she squinted through the formidable wire mesh covering her window. I might manage to remove that over time, she thought, but only with a strong file and tools for leverage. But in addition there were the bars painted white. Though she doubted whether she had the strength required to file through them, she liked to look and think of every possibility. She had been a devotee of detective novels from childhood and her imagination was stirring. Inspired by her observation of the main gate, she was eager to take in every aspect of her environment, inside the lock-up and beyond. She wondered whether she would be allowed out to exercise but decided against asking that question too soon.

19

That afternoon Eleanor spent an enjoyable time playing rummy with her new-found friends. They were a quick-talking, street-wise group who had clearly lived their lives on the edge. Most of all, she was keen to hear their views about Fort Napier. But in the first place to explain why they were confined like common criminals in the lock-up.

'Well, my heart,' Swanny explained to her new best friend, while the cards were dealt. 'We've all been in open asylums to try and dry out, but you know, if it's easy to slip into town and get just the one drink you're craving, then that's the instant road to ruin. It just don't work.'

'Just that teeny, weeny tot of the golden fluid,' Francina cut in. 'If there's an open door or window, even three storeys up, you'll shin down the nearest drainpipe and not even the American marines will prevent you reaching your target.'

'It's lock and key for us,' Swanny continued. 'It's the only solution. We get signed in for a minimum of three months. If we don't sign ourselves in, our families have that power. "Go dry out!" they say. And it's the only way out for the likes of us.

'It's my third time here in five years. The treatment can vary. But it's mainly medication and some psychological stuff. You know, they try to motivate you like they do at Alcoholics Anonymous.'

'There's also something called aversion therapy', Francina explained. 'You get electric shock treatment. But they had some bad results here with patients going into convulsions and one or two dying. So they stopped it.'

'Stopped that?' Swanny cut in bitterly. 'That'll be the frosty Friday. It's an open secret that they're experimenting on the blacks, particularly at Weskoppies in Pretoria. Maybe here too.'

Eleanor thought of Wentworth, and the House of Truth, of Shadrack Mapumulo and the electric torture treatment the Special Branch were using. She realised that they would certainly be learning from the state psychiatrists and vice versa.

As they started on a new round of rummy, Eleanor found herself delighting in the old familiar game, the comforting pattern of building matching suits of cards and their sequences along with the thrill of winning a hand. They played with matchsticks and chain-smoked. Sometimes politics came up in unexpected ways as when, to Eleanor's astonishment, they referred to the joker as 'Dr Verwoerd'.

'Why's that?' she enquired.

Francina, who had just played the joker card to win a round, answered, 'Because he's giving the *munts* all the land back. My folk live in the Transkei, from way back. He's talking of making it a Bantustan – a damn independent state for the black man. What a joke!'

The others concurred, except Swanny, who said, 'Well, we've got to give the native something. Otherwise there'll be constant unrest. No, I think of Verwoerd as a joker because he believes he is such a smart arse laying down one new law

86

after another. He's putting this whole land into a mental and physical straitjacket.'

'Well,' said Eleanor, as they looked her way for a contribution, 'unless everyone has a fair deal, we'll never sort out our problems, will we? And I don't think we should simply leave things for our children to solve because they will only get worse if nothing is done. If someone like Harold Macmillan talked in our Parliament just three years ago about a wind of change sweeping through Africa, then surely we need to fall in step?' She could not afford to create animosity and had decided not to be too radical. She looked at Swanny and asked, 'Are you saying something like that?'

'Exactly,' was the reply. 'My father used to say that an empty belly always leads to trouble. You know, idle hands do the devil's work. There's too much hunger and unemployment in this country.'

The quietest of the quartet piped up: 'Yes, too many of us whites are unemployed. At least Verwoerd's party will look after the white man.'

'And the white woman?' Swanny asked.

'If the man's got work, then we've got food on the table, and Johnnie Walker if we're good.'

'And Turkish delight at bedtime. Ooooh, bring me that Turk!' the quiet one unexpectedly cut in, to peals of laughter.

Eleanor adapted smoothly to the regime of the six o'clock wake-up, with staff engrossed in getting the drugged patients out of bed; the morning wash; the institutional meals; the twice-daily administration of medication to the inmates, who stood in line docilely and swallowed fistfuls of pills; the petty squabbles among them and the grumblings of the staff. These were all working-class white women who on occasion could get rough when a patient became violent. She would then be dragged off to one of the padded cells, placed in a straitjacket and given an injection, which put her out cold for a couple of days.

Eleanor was well behaved and greeted the staff politely. They consequently roped her in to help with the small chores like laying the tables and handing out clean towels to the patients once a week. In time she had freedom of movement anywhere inside the prison during the day.

There were some Africans who worked in the lock-up for whites. They were cleaners, female inmates from the segregated black section, who were entrusted with the task because whites were not expected to clean up their own mess. Eleanor marvelled at the way in which the culture of 'white South Africa' was reflected within the walls of Fort Napier, right down to the lock-up for the dangerous psychotics. Not for the first time did she reflect that insanity in South Africa was not confined within the walls of a mental asylum. She thought of the irrational race laws Dr Verwoerd's government had passed, of the trigger-happy police and psychopaths like Grobler in the Special Branch, of the whites on the Durban bus who could not tolerate Africans sitting too close to them though they entrusted their children to their care. Where then was the true madness?

Once over a lively hand of rummy Francina remarked sagely: 'You've got to keep an eye on these *munts*. They're clever at thieving from us.' Eleanor soon saw what this meant. While she was walking down a corridor being cleaned by a small, emaciated African woman in her fifties, in green dust-coat and matching *doek*, and was smoking a cigarette, she barely felt the woman touch her arm. As she turned to look, the cigarette was being whipped away from between her fingers. It was all done so effortlessly, as if by a magician, and she caught her breath in surprise as the woman audaciously puffed smoke rings her way, cackling like an old hen.

Because of a shortage of white staff, an African nurse would deliver medication from the hospital's dispensary several times a week. Eleanor greeted her respectfully and warmly as *dadewethu* (sister) instead of the customary *meid* (maid), which was the derogatory term employed by most whites. As a result, whenever she appeared she gave Eleanor a sympathetic nod. On one occasion when Eleanor was worrying about her escape plan, she decided to test her views.

'Do you know why I'm here?' she asked.

'You're in trouble with the police?'

'Yes, the political police. It's because my friends are ANC.'

'Shame,' she replied. 'We know whites like you help us. The country is bad. I know there are boys from my township who have gone to Bechuanaland to become freedom fighters.'

Eleanor was encouraged by her response but did not want to take things any further at that point. She had to be cautious. She simply asked her name. 'I'm Precious,' the woman replied.

20

Eleanor learnt over cards that the monthly event not to be missed was a dance involving males and females from the prison wards. A special concession was made for Eleanor when it was agreed that owing to her good behaviour she could go along to watch proceedings.

Saturday after lunch, the females all lined up to get a dab of powder on each cheek and a smudge of red lipstick. There were oohs and ahs as they were made pretty as if for a pantomime, and they were allowed to wear their civilian dresses, which were generally cheap floral prints much the worse for wear. But they could have been preparing for a mayoral ball, so proud and happy they were.

Eleanor joined the staff as they escorted the excited inmates through a rear door, and across a grass verge, to what must have been a drill hall in the days of the British garrison. It had a wooden floor and panelled walls adorned with the military crests of colonial regiments from the War of 1879 when the British empire had loosed anarchy on the Zulu kingdom in the name of the civilising mission.

The men, all dressed in an assortment of cast-away suits and patched-up jackets and ties, were sitting in chairs along one side of the hall. Eleanor was sure some wore cast-off military tunics. The women in their faded frocks took their seats on the other side facing the men. Everyone sat stiff and still, on their best behaviour. A nurse wound up an old-fashioned gramophone player and placed a 78 rpm vinyl record on the turntable. The moment the music ground out, every inmate, man and woman, sprang to their feet with alacrity and raced forward. Those more alert had already decided who to choose to dance with and had sat down opposite their partner according to a well-established pattern. They consequently found their opposite number without trouble. The less alert, on the other hand, stumbled around in confusion until they grabbed whoever was available and struggled to catch up with the dance step. It was good old-fashioned *tickey-draai*. The male extended his left arm rigidly up and to the side, while holding his partner's right arm outwards. The woman's arm would be vigorously pumped up and down as though it was a handle. At the same time the man's other arm would be pressed into the crook of his partner's lower back while she clutched his shoulder. In this stylised manner they would stride in stiff fashion swiftly across the floor, striving to keep time with the music. At times when the pace of the music increased in tempo they almost galloped around the hall. At last, when the music ended they broke apart without a word and retreated back to their chairs, waiting patiently for the next dance.

Eleanor was fascinated. Apart from their strange expressions, the so-called psychotically insane showed signs of positive social behaviour. She saw the potential for scientific therapy if only there was a different treatment regime. She mused at the way the lives of these men and women were being wasted by years of incarceration without meaningful treatment. And these were whites. What of the mentally disturbed Africans? Guinea pigs for the toxic mix of new drugs and for electro-convulsive therapy, she guessed.

The afternoon passed by extremely pleasantly without incident, and that evening everyone ate their dinner and went to sleep in a calm and happy state.

After observing the dance, it struck Eleanor that getting the inmates interested in drawing and painting would benefit them enormously. She raised this with the Superintendent and volunteered to supervise lessons, explaining that she had been an art student at college. He and the Matron could see the positive value of her suggestion, but as with everything else there was the budgetary issue. Where, for example, would they get funds for paper, paint, brushes? Eleanor suggested that they start off with a pilot project involving six patients. All they required would be six sketch pads, crayons and pencils. They were both drawn in by Eleanor's enthusiasm. It was no matter that the Super saw himself getting credit for the initiative. Who knew, maybe there would be palpable improvements in behaviour and even research and a case study to follow? It was decided that the initial cost would be so small that Matron could draw on her petty cash account. To Eleanor's delight, the project was approved.

Soon six rather bemused women, a mixture of young and old, were seated at a large table with Eleanor. The Matron watched with interest. On her own pad Eleanor showed the class how to hold a crayon, make a circle and gently colour it in with a crayon of choice. She invited them to do likewise. Two of them did so with the necessary skill. Three others failed to get going after breaking the crayons by exerting too much pressure.

92

The sixth, a pretty, young brunette with pigtails called Belinda, whom Eleanor had never seen talking or smiling, ignored what had been suggested and began effortlessly to draw a picture. After Eleanor had shown the disappointed trio how to hold their crayons more gently, she looked to see how the young woman was progressing. The picture that materialised was of a large house surrounded by trees. Storm clouds were gathering. The colours were dark and ominous. She picked up an orange crayon and with a deft stroke added a fork of lightning. She made a yellow figure appear in an upstairs window and pencilled in black hair and pigtails and an open mouth but no eyes. The arms of the figure were raised as if screaming for help. She reached for a red crayon and surrounded the figure in flames. The fire spread rapidly until the whole house was ablaze. Eleanor and the Matron were transfixed. Without turning a hair, the young woman tore up her drawing into little pieces. 'Oh, no Belinda, don't do that!' said Matron. 'You draw and colour with talent,' chimed Eleanor. 'Would you like to draw something else?' But Belinda sat expressionless, her arms folded, while the rest of the class were preoccupied in trying out the effects of the different coloured crayons.

'Most interesting,' Matron observed when the first lesson was concluded. 'They did indeed seem to enjoy that. And I can't wait to inform Belinda's psychiatrist about that drawing. He has been trying to get her to express herself since the court ordered an assessment of her mental condition last month. She's on trial for burning her house down with her young children inside. They died of asphyxiation and she was pulled out unconscious by the firemen. She had taken an overdose and clearly meant to take her own life. Her husband was having an affair with her sister and had left home.'

Soon Eleanor had both the Superintendent and Matron fully behind the art project. One hour a day was devoted to the lessons, and before the week was up an emboldened Eleanor suggested that they be allowed out to draw the trees, flowers and blue sky outside. 'Let's see if we can coax Belinda to express herself outdoors. The fresh air and sunshine might inspire her to renewed and possibly happier efforts. Besides, it will be interesting to observe what gets reflected in the art of the other women.' Eleanor could see that the Superintendent was ready to agree. But he looked Eleanor directly in the eye and said, 'You must promise you will not try to run away.'

'Superintendent, I would never use an art class to do something like that. I promise.'

The trip around the grounds, to draw flowers and trees and glimpses of distant hills, acted like a tonic on pupils and teacher alike. Eleanor could see how beneficial the therapy was for her class. Like children, they gained great pleasure from their naive drawings and especially from Eleanor's praise. But still Belinda's interest failed to reignite. Locked within her own skull, she refused to release the initial demon she had momentarily revealed. Eleanor hoped that somehow they might be able to help this tragic young woman, who could so easily end up in a lifetime of sedation in the Fort Napier lock-up. As for her, the sooner she could get out of the place the better.

She lay in bed, her mind focused on Fort Napier's lay-out and what she had been able to observe outside. From the time of her arrival she had seen how extensive Fort Napier was, with many buildings and a road system leading to the main gate, from where the road ran downhill into Pietermaritzburg. There were numerous paths that were used by patients and staff alike. She noted that the busiest time appeared to be around the change of shift at six in the morning and again at five in the afternoon. Lunchtime, too, was busy.

She analysed the security process at the main gate. The security guards appeared to pay attention only to those in vehicles and would give just cursory glances at those on foot. Why should they think anyone was being smuggled out anyway? It was only a break-out from the internal prison that could pose a threat, but the inmates there were under secure lock and key. She began to see that the big challenge lay in getting out of the lock-up undetected, at least for thirty minutes before the alarm could be raised, to give her the chance of brazenly walking right through the main gate with other staff members and visitors. After that she faced a brisk walk into town, where she would have to be promptly picked up by waiting comrades. She would also need a disguise of sorts and some money in case she had to jump into a taxi or make a telephone call in the town. She laid a dress that she had not worn under her mattress with a pale yellow scarf to cover her head. Together with these she secreted a used cigarette packet into which she placed a black crayon from the art class and a red lipstick used on the inmates for the dance. These would do for make-up when the time came. Finally, she desperately needed contact with the underground and decided on the student group at the local university. Perhaps she could get to them through her friend Swanny.

21

Rummy with Swanny and company had become her main form of relaxation and, she hoped, her life-line. All four women were permitted visitors although these were infrequent. Eleanor found an opportunity to raise with Swanny the possibility of a visit from a friend. Would she write a letter to a student named Rob at the university and invite him to visit a lonely woman who needed company? Eleanor banked on Rob reacting positively, if anything out of sheer curiosity. She was relieved when Swanny unhesitatingly agreed. Eleanor dictated a letter that ended: 'Please come and visit. Either you or someone of your faith.' To the hospital authorities this would appear to refer to a simple matter of religion. Eleanor banked on the hope that Rob, an atheist, would sense a hidden signal and not ignore the letter.

Within the week a nurse informed Swanny as lunch ended that there was a visitor for her in the waiting room. Swanny nodded to Eleanor, who slipped away to her room where she had prepared two letters on very thin cigarette-box paper. One was for the underground comrades; the other for Ronnie. She waited anxiously for a few minutes wondering whether she would be able to slip into the waiting room unnoticed and pass her letters to Rob, who by now should be in conversation with Swanny. As she walked past, she was relieved to see Swanny seated with her guest. The coast was clear and there were no staff members in sight. Taking her chance, Eleanor walked into the room and placed her hand lightly on the visitor's shoulder. It was Rob alright, fresh-faced and pink-cheeked. He turned and went pale with shock as he recognised her: 'My God, Eleanor,' he stuttered. She slipped him her letters, turned on her heel, and was out in a flash. When she got to her room, she sat on her bed and lit a cigarette, her hands shaking.

The letters were brief, similar and to the point. She recounted her arrest, gave details of what was going on at the Wentworth interrogation centre, and most importantly recorded her suspicions about Bruno Mtolo. She explained how she had gone on hunger strike and been transferred to Fort Napier for assessment. The letter to the Pietermaritzburg group appealed for assistance:

'I believe I have a fairly good chance of escaping from here before they take me back to prison. Rob will see how easy it is to come and go from this place because, after all, it is a vast mental home open to the families and friends of patients and any number of visitors, staff and service delivery people. It is only my section that consists of a lock-up and is sealed off like any prison. I believe I can get out of here, and then into town. What I am asking is permission to make the break and for a car to be available to pick me up. It could be something like thirty minutes before my absence is noted. Could Rob come back in a week at the utmost and slip me a note with instructions via my friend who has written to him? She is in here for voluntary treatment, not a mental patient, and I believe I can rely on her. I don't think I have much more than a couple of weeks at the most, so please hurry. Be assured I am in total control of my

Rob Anderson as a student.

faculties, am dead serious about the prospect of escape and am quite sane!'

The letter to Ronnie was in similar vein but with more detail about Grobler and his determination to track Ronnie down and her concern for his safety. She concluded:

'It was easy to feign a mental breakdown. I'm in a lock-up with about 70 poor wretches. Some are completely round the bend but it's surprising how quickly one gets used to this sort of thing. I've made contact with some sympathetic people here, and it's possible to escape. I don't know how long the SB will tolerate my presence here. It's supposed to be temporary.'

At the end she added XXXs and QQQs for kisses and hugs

and the words 'till all the seas run dry'. The Q represented a hug with a hand pressed into the small of the back, the way she liked him to hug her.

Eleanor longed to be free – free of her dread of the Special Branch and the prospect of returning to Grobler's clutches before very long. The psychiatric assessment could surely not take more than a month. Rob and company had to act speedily. She feared breaking under interrogation if placed once more at the mercy of the SB or, more probably, giving away sensitive information as a result of hallucinating in solitary confinement. There were plenty of examples of this in the resistance literature of the Second World War she had loved to read as a teenager. And it was a point of conjecture that the Special Branch would soon start using truth drugs. She had so much information that she had to conceal at all costs. If she broke down, she would never be able to live with herself.

It was late on a Friday afternoon. She was helping a nurse with the laundry and was in a subdued mood, fretting because a week had gone by since Rob's visit to Swanny and there had been no response to her letters.

'Eleanor, you're looking quite pale today.'

'Am I?' she responded.

'Yes. And what's happened to your mood? Matron's been saying how cheerful you've been and how helpful with the patients. We will miss you.'

'Miss me? What do you mean?'

The answer ran like a blade through her heart: 'Matron says the police are coming to fetch you on Monday morning.'

22

Eleanor did her best not to respond or reveal her shock. Fortunately they had folded the last of the newly laundered towels. She said she hoped the nurse would have a relaxed weekend and hastened away. Her heart was beating wildly and she was desperate to locate Precious, the African nurse who sometimes assisted in the lock-up section. Fortunately she had seen her little more than an hour before, attending to grocery supplies in the kitchen. In a state bordering on panic, Eleanor found her still there. This was the time to take her chance and she hoped her luck would hold.

'Precious, I need your help, urgently.'

She looked at Eleanor with wide eyes.

Eleanor told her that the Special Branch would be taking her back to prison on Monday. 'I need to get out of here before then,' she said. 'Will you help me?'

'I've been thinking about you,' Precious replied. 'The boys in the township told me that we must help any *umlungu* who is with us and against the Boers. They say a person like you is a comrade.'

She continued: 'Be ready tomorrow morning at six sharp. I will leave the back door unlocked, but just for five minutes. You must slip out then. I will leave a small basket on the inside by the door. A lot of the staff carry baskets like that for their things. Change your appearance if you can and walk through the grounds like any staff member and out of the gate. Just ignore the security guards. They don't bother anyone walking out.'

'The main gate?' Eleanor asked breathlessly.

'The main gate. Lots of staff will be coming and going. Just hope you're not recognised. Now go quick before we're seen.'

Eleanor tearfully embraced her.

23

Eleanor hardly slept all night. Would the plan work? Would Precious be true to her word and unlock the rear door at six? Once out, would she be spotted walking through the grounds of Fort Napier?

And what about the main gate? That would be the next big challenge. Could she get past the security guards or would they stop her? That prospect worried her particularly. But she had managed to steal a letterhead from Matron's office. Tonight she would write a note indicating that she was a staff member and would append the Superintendent's signature. She was sure that security personnel at the gate would have no idea what his signature looked like. Having that note would provide insurance in case she was stopped. It would also bolster her sense of confidence.

And then, once out, would she manage to get into town before the alarm was sounded? The staff would be preoccupied with the inmates, who were such a handful at that time of the morning. But before long her absence from breakfast would be noted. She worked out that it would take her almost ten minutes to get out of the asylum grounds, and she would need a minimum of ten minutes to get down a side road into town, for she must avoid the main road. She would need another ten minutes or so to find a shop, hopefully an Indian store, which generally opened early, to make a call to the comrades to come and fetch her.

By that time breakfast would be over and, if somehow they had not already noticed she was missing, they would certainly discover she had absconded by then. The whole of Pietermaritzburg would be put on alert. Could she be off the streets and in a safe place by then? It all sounded like a tall order, but she felt it was attainable. No pulling out now, she mused. The die is cast and I must seize the opportunity. It was all up to Precious.

All night she tossed and turned. By five she was up and putting on the dress she had hidden under the mattress. It was a simple light-green cotton frock with sleeves, which looked well pressed from being carefully laid out under the mattress. She would take her woollen grey cardigan but not wear it because she had often been seen in it. Instead she would put it in the basket that Precious would leave by the door. Once outside, she would wrap her scarf around her head. She had the ten rand note she had smuggled out of her Durban cottage and a few coins for the public telephone box. These she had 'borrowed' from the card players when they were not looking. She applied the lipstick and used some to colour her cheeks as well, for she was extremely pale. She used the crayon from the art class to darken her eyebrows. She had not applied make-up since arriving at Fort Napier.

As the hands of her watch approached six, she began to hear the first stirrings of the inmates. She hoped they had not been overdosed the evening before. Any prolonged difficulty waking them could jeopardise the timing of her arrangement with Precious. She heard a nurse doing the rounds, calling to this or that inmate to wake up, and waited anxiously for her cell to be unlocked. It was normally opened before six. Eleanor was fretting: she felt she would faint if the woman was held up by someone and delayed in opening her cell in time. With a shudder she realised that she had not accounted for the one factor on which everything now hinged, and that was being out of her cell and at the rear door, which Precious could only afford to keep unlocked until five past six. She heard the nurse advancing down the passage. After what seemed an eternity, she reaching the door of her cell, where she struggled to find the correct key. It was already after six. 'Oh, nurse,' Eleanor called out, 'I'm dying to go to the toilet. Please hurry.'

The nurse at last found the correct key and unlocked the cell door. Eleanor had slipped on her gown to hide her dress and lay on her bed with her back to the door in case the nurse glanced in. It was three minutes past six and time was running out fast. After waiting for thirty seconds for the nurse to disappear, Eleanor crept out quickly and silently. She saw some patients already rising in the main dormitory and moved swiftly along a passage which led to the rear of the building. She almost rushed to the iron door. Her heart leapt with excitement when she saw that Precious had left a basket for her. She stashed the gown and cardigan into it and then threw the scarf deftly around her head and shoulders. She turned the door handle, heard a satisfying click, and pushed it open. As she stepped outside, she was dazzled by the sunlight.

24

She half expected a trap, fearing that Grobler would be waiting for her. But there was the sheer relief of the early morning calm, the innocent chirping of birds and a powder-blue sky. Struggling to keep from running, she walked at a swift pace in the direction of the gate. She got a shock as a police car drove by but the uniformed man at the wheel paid no attention to her. She saw him dropping off a woman passenger at one of the hostels, execute a U-turn and head back to the exit. There were staff members walking in that direction and others arriving, some in cars. Precious had been observant about the basket and Eleanor felt she fitted into the scene.

As she came within sight of the main gate, she saw a big truck arriving and two security guards both approached it. She stepped up her pace, hoping to reach the exit while the guards were preoccupied with the driver. As she reached the gate, two other guards came out from their sentry point and one stopped a woman pedestrian ahead of her. The thought that the alarm had been raised terrified her because, if so, she would surely be captured at that point. She nervously fingered the letter with the Superintendent's forged signature. To her relief a friendly conversation was in progress and she realised the security man knew the staff member. She walked right by, hearing them talking about a rugby match. The other guard had gone back into the sentry post and the two others were still involved with the driver of the truck. She was over the threshold of Fort Napier; she was out of captivity. It was unbelievable.

She walked on down the hill, speeding up to walk just behind three off-duty nurses ahead of her. With every step she took she expected a barked command from behind ordering her to stop in her tracks or the wailing of a siren and an ambulance catching up with her. But nothing happened. Within a few minutes she branched off the main road and began walking as fast as possible down a side road into the town. At a corner she spotted an ambulance racing down the main road, its siren wailing. That must be for me, she thought; I must keep cool and not run. Thank goodness the area she was in was deserted.

Tense and breathless, she came to an Asian corner shop, relieved that it was open. An old man in a knitted Muslim skull-cap eyed her dolefully and bade her good morning. It was not often that a white person came into his store. She asked for a cold drink and held out her ten rand note: 'I need to make a telephone call urgently. Please help me!'

'Is it a local call?' he asked, and she nodded. He showed her where his telephone was. She was pleased that its position provided some privacy, more especially that it was in a nook shielded from the door of the shop. If anyone came looking for her, she would rush out the back way or even ask the shopkeeper to hide her.

She knew the number by heart and hoped it would be answered. She heard the sleepy voice of a man enquiring who was telephoning.

'Me ... me ...' she answered, hoping he would recognise her

106

voice, 'your friend from Durban.'

'Who? Who's that?'

He was hard of hearing, English was not his first language and she had to speak up. 'I gave Rob a letter last week. It's me. I got out of hospital. I need you to fetch me.'

'You! Yes, of course, where? Where are you?' She could tell he understood and was well aware of the need to reach her urgently.

She asked the shopkeeper the name of the street and relayed this to her friend. He told her he would be there in his green Mini within ten minutes.

The minutes ticked by. She fiddled around with the goods on display. The shopkeeper asked if she would like some samoosas with her Coke but she declined. Ten minutes became fifteen. Where could her friend be? She suddenly realised this was a corner shop and she had only given him one street name. So she slipped out and darted to the corner. Almost miraculously she saw the green Mini doing a U-turn down the road and went running after it. Luckily the driver spotted her and did a quick manoeuvre, the vehicle screeching up to her. 'Jump in!' he shouted. She needed no such bidding. He explained that for the last five minutes he had been driving up and down the street.

She would always remember him in his gown and slippers and the way he had immediately responded to her call. He was a Portuguese postgraduate student at the university and came from Lourenço Marques, in neighbouring Mozambique. He was the leader of Rob's unit. He had an impressive grasp of Marxist theory, seemed to be steeped in the folklore of European communism. She had always regarded him as the quintessence of an underground conspirator. His name was Pedro and it was he who had picked up Ebrahim and Ronnie when they fled from Hillcrest. He kept shaking his head in disbelief, his eyes vigilant for signs of police cars as he engaged the gears of his Mini Minor and drove off as on a speedway track. 'Amazing! You've done it. Single-handedly you've beaten them.' It was 22 September, five weeks since her arrest at Griggs bookstore, and four weeks since her incarceration in Fort Napier mental asylum.

25

They drove straight to his house in a middle-class suburb, entering by way of the garage. It was a strange, almost dream-like sensation, being in an elegant home after her five-week ordeal. All Eleanor wanted to do was collapse on a sofa with a cigarette and a cup of tea.

'Oh Penny,' she said to Pedro's wife, 'if you have Earl Grey I'd love that. Nice and strong. After Fort Napier I could do with a bit of TLC.'

Penny embraced her warmly and told her she deserved all the 'tender loving care' in the world. But privately Penny was worried: Pedro's mother from Lourenço Marques was staying with them. She had arrived to help out with Pedro and Penny's new-born daughter. Coming from the Portuguese colony under Salazar's fascist regime, with its dreaded secret police, the PIDE, she was alarmed at what she sensed was going on and, with Eleanor's arrival, had collapsed. Penny had to revive her with smelling salts and put her to bed.

Rob soon arrived. It was explained that Eleanor's letters had indeed been delivered to Bram and Ronnie, who was in Johannesburg. They were impressed that she had wheedled her way into Fort Napier. Bram had instructed them to do everything possible to help her escape and they had been attending to various details, such as carrying out a thorough

Pedro with Eleanor and Ronnie in 2003.

reconnaissance of Fort Napier and following up a lead with somebody's cousin who worked there. They were also trying to check up on Mrs Swanepoel (Swanny), in case she was a police plant. And Rob was intending to visit Fort Napier in the coming week. Eleanor groaned inwardly, secretly relieved that she had not had to wait for them to get their plan together. Rob explained that he had nearly ignored the letter. He had even sought advice from a lecturer in the Psychology Department, who advised him to stay away. It was the reference to 'someone of your faith' that had finally got through to him.

'Of course,' Pedro cut in, 'we have to get you away from here as soon as possible. It's not at all safe.'

Rob explained that police cars and Fort Napier ambulances were racing around town, clearly on the look-out for her. Some comrades were checking the main road to Durban and

Johannesburg for roadblocks, which they thought would soon be in place. They expected the SB to raid the houses of all known sympathisers and especially the university residences.

As a postgraduate student Pedro had managed to keep a low profile and avoid being seen in public in the company of Rob and the others. However, even his place was considered not safe enough and there was the complication of his mother's presence. It was decided that they needed to shift Eleanor by nightfall. The problem was, where to? While this was being thought through, Eleanor raised the question of her appearance.

'The first thing I need is to change the colour of my hair. Someone please get me a bottle of black hair dye from the chemist. And Penny, dear, can you cut my hair short, very short?'

Penny was rather like Eleanor and had always admired her. 'You never cease to amaze me,' she said. 'Here you are after such a gruelling, awful ordeal, with half the police force after you, chirping away so cheerfully.' She laughed. 'Drinking cup after cup of my Earl Grey tea. Such an unlikely fugitive! Who would believe you've been so involved in all this secrecy?'

While her soft, fair curls were being snipped away, someone had the idea of disguising Eleanor as a boy. She was not too happy about this. How would she pass close inspection? And what if she had to speak? She stressed that one needed to be comfortable in a disguise so as to be able to act naturally. Yes, they pointed out, but the police were looking for a woman. They would not bother with a car filled with men. She could practise talking right away. They would coach her. 'Come on, Eleanor, you of all people can do it.' After a short debate she could see the merits of their argument. They took her measurements and Rob went off to shop for the hair dye and clothing. She was worried about the shoe size. 'My feet are very narrow, bear that in mind, please,' was her one request.

By afternoon the transformation of Eleanor into a young high-school boy was under way. She looked boyishly attractive with a short urchin cut. The black hair colour suited her and greatly changed her appearance. She still felt apprehensive about carrying off the male role. Though she thought that if she dressed in teenage female clothing she would not be recognised by her own mother, she decided against reopening the debate. She would simply grit her teeth, go through the gender change and hope she did not have to talk to strangers. She changed into the male clothing in the bathroom. The shirt was a little large but would do. The trousers were similarly too large at the waist but, by tightening the belt, she got them to stay up well enough. The jacket was fine but the shoes were too wide and uncomfortable, so her flat-heeled brown moccasins would have to suffice. At least they were appropriate if she needed to run. She knotted a plain tie around her neck but still was unsure. It was when she put on a school cap Rob had bought that she felt more confident.

She walked into the lounge and, in the deepest voice she could muster, addressed them: 'Good day, I'll have a pint of beer, please.'

There was laughter and applause. 'And gimme another fag, will you,' she added, jutting out her jaw and affecting a gangster-like tone. Her levity could be relied on in the tensest of situations.

The report about police deployment had come in. It

confirmed that all points around Pietermaritzburg were ringed with roadblocks, with the main concentration on the Durban–Johannesburg highway. Police had already raided the female residence at the university and searched the rooms. Rob pointed out that he could drive Eleanor along a township road and from there use a dirt track that connected with a minor road to Zululand to the north-east. It would be a long, arduous detour but they could head off in that direction and then cut back west to meet the Johannesburg road north of Ladysmith.

Eleanor came up with another option. 'As much as I would love to get to Jo'burg as soon as possible, the main road even beyond Ladysmith might not be so safe at present. I have a friend in Zululand who I think would put me up for a few days, until the heat cools down. What do you say?'

This sounded a most sensible solution to them. 'OK then,' Pedro summed up. 'Rob will drive you away as soon as it's dark. We will inform our friends in Jo'burg that you are free but that you will only be with them in several days' time. Coming after Goldreich's and Wolpe's escape in August, this is another blow against the Special Branch and the government.'

26

Eleanor tried shielding her eyes from the policeman's torch. Even though they had taken the township route, they were stopped at a check-point after all. A second policeman on the driver's side was shining his torch at Rob and enquiring in a suspicious voice why they were on the road 'to the kaffir township'.

'I'm afraid we're lost, officer,' he replied in a tense voice.

'Where are you going?'

'My young brother and I are on our way to a family wedding in Greytown. It's tomorrow. We're from Maritzburg. I've been trying to get to that road. I must have taken a wrong turn.'

He too shone his torch at Eleanor. Two pairs of police eyes were looking at her. She accentuated her squint in the hope of altering her appearance as much as possible and coughed as deeply as she could.

The policeman told Rob to take the very next turn right, to proceed for three miles to a junction with a garage, and then take the left turn. 'That's the road you need to be on. Just steer clear of the township ahead. A kaffir will slit your throat for ten bob. And tonight's Saturday. They're *moerse dronk* and anything goes.'

The two drove on in silence. Rob wondered whether it was a routine Saturday night check but concluded they must be on the look-out for Eleanor. Tension and weariness were taking their toll. She said nothing, feeling awfully tired, but sat bolt upright, peering into the road ahead, petrified they would be stopped again.

The drive along the rutted, sandy road, for which Rob's car was ill suited, was dreadful. Even worse, he kept taking the wrong turn and getting lost. What should have taken four hours became six and then in the small hours of the morning the radiator began to boil over. They had to keep stopping to let it cool down. First light found them stuck on the side of the road near a farmhouse in the middle of sugarcane fields and rolling Zululand hills dotted with traditional beehive-shaped huts and homesteads.

A ruddy-faced farmer came out to investigate. 'Car break-down?' he asked Rob, who explained that the radiator kept boiling over. 'Could be the thermostat,' the farmer replied in a knowledgeable way. 'There's a garage ten miles up the road that does repairs, but they only open at eight. I can ring them then for you.' He looked from Rob to Eleanor and enquired hospitably: 'If you boys need a wash-up and cuppa tea, you're welcome to come into the farmhouse.'

As they followed him Eleanor whispered to Rob that under no circumstances was he to accept breakfast if offered. She thought he looked a bit dejected as she made the point.

They were ushered into a large, old-fashioned bathroom with toilet. She was a bit grouchy with Rob because he had got into a very convivial conversation with the farmer and feared he was opening them up for a closer interaction than she wanted. She also felt he should have checked the water in the car's radiator before leaving on such an arduous journey.

Perhaps it was more her nerves but she snapped at him: 'I'll go first on the loo. You go into the corner, turn your head away, and block your ears.'

When they had relieved themselves and washed, they found the farmer, joined by his beaming wife and young son, ready to invite them to sit down for breakfast. Rob readily accepted while Eleanor declined, stroking her stomach and mumbling in a low voice: 'Upset tummy. I need fresh air.'

The woman sat her down outside on the *stoep* and said she would make her a mug of strong black tea: 'Best thing for a tummy upset.' The offer was gratefully accepted by Eleanor, who nodded her head vigorously.

She sipped her tea and lit a cigarette, inhaling deeply. She sniggered when she heard the farmer saying to the pink-cheeked Rob: 'Isn't the fellow too young to be smoking?'

'Oh, he's not that young. He's eighteen,' was the reply.

'Lanky lad,' the farmer observed. 'Make a good fast bowler. Would need to put on weight.'

A mechanic from the garage arrived in a truck and towed Rob's car into town. They sat in the cab with him. Once again Eleanor pretended to be feeling ill, regretting her masculine disguise. The problem turned out to be a faulty thermostat and it was afternoon before the car would be ready. Rob sat with her while she had brunch in a fly-blown café that served a plate of greasy bacon, eggs and *boerewors*. She was ravenous and consumed it all with more tea. While she was in the middle of the meal the farmer looked in and waved at Rob: 'Glad he's got his appetite back.' Rob had a pack of cards in his car and she played patience in the café while he chatted to the garage owner about racing cars.

While they were at Pedro's she had had the foresight to look up her friend's telephone number. He was a ranger at Imfolozi game park several hours away. She phoned from the café and waited patiently for him to come on the line. 'Hello, Hugh,' she said. 'This is Jimmy and Helen's daughter.' She did not want to use her name in case of being overheard. 'Eleanor,' he said, 'have the cops released you?' She told him she would fill him in soon, because she was in the vicinity. Could she come and visit for a few days. 'Of course,' he replied. Eleanor had to caution him: 'Hugh, don't talk about this and please don't even think of phoning my folks. Nobody is to know. I trust there's nobody there who knows me?'

He immediately realised that something was going on and told her to arrive after dark. 'I will be at the security gate at 7 pm waiting for you.'

They arrived near the game park under a crimson sunset. She and Rob sat in his car watching the magic colour changes of mauves, pinks and purples across sky and landscape in the crystal-cool stillness of the African bush. The silence and solitude were like a soothing balm and she felt the gentleness envelop her. The conflict in the country, the raids and arrests, the gruesome torture of detainees, the pathetic inmates of Fort Napier, the waste of life generation after generation, all could have been taking place on another planet, so indifferent nature seemed to the plight of humanity. It was as though she had never been incarcerated. The twilight was short and the dark descended rapidly. Soon the clear night sky was aglitter in mesmerising starlight. It was time to rendezvous with Hugh, the game ranger.

Hugh was waiting and she thanked Rob, who without

further ado drove off smartly. It was better for the sake of security that the two men did not meet.

Hugh Dent was a young, sun-tanned ranger. He was a friend of Eleanor's art teacher, Harold Strachan, and son of a close friend of Alan Paton. She knew Hugh was something of an old-style liberal and committed Christian. She explained that she had escaped from Fort Napier and was on the run and needed somewhere to lie low for a few days. He told her that while there were many visitors in the main camp, there were just a couple of young women staff members, learning the routines, at an isolated satellite camp and she would be joining them. However, there was no way, in that kind of proximity, that she could fool them with her masculine disguise. She was more than happy to agree and immediately changed into a pair of slacks and a blouse Penny had given her.

They jumped into Hugh's vehicle and rode into the park. After a short drive they came to a halt. He explained that they could only reach the satellite camp by foot and took her hand as they came to a stream. They had to wade through in total darkness. He carried her on his back, using a hefty stick to feel the way carefully forward. Afterwards he explained that there was always the off-chance that they could step on a sleeping crocodile. She thought he was joking but he assured her he was dead serious.

The camp was rudimentary and consisted of two small tents and a dining enclosure with shower and toilet. Two young women, training to become staff members, were in the process of preparing a meal on an open fire. Hugh introduced Eleanor as a special guest who would be with them for a couple of days. After Eleanor washed, she joined them for an appetising meal

118

of warthog stew and baked potatoes. They served brandy and Coke to go with it and Eleanor enjoyed the relaxing surge of the alcohol. They talked about the wonders of the bush and the Zulu country and Eleanor soon wished them goodnight.

The next day Hugh joined them on an invigorating hike through the park to view the game at close quarters and lecture them on the habits of the animals, recognition of their spoor, the vegetation that the rhinoceros, elephant and other species preferred, and the characteristics of the flora. Eleanor found all the activity a tonic for her nerves and again felt the complexity of the country called South Africa with its contrast between the most sublime nature and the horrors that were taking place elsewhere.

Most whites, like the two pleasant women she was with, seemed to live in another country, judging from the chit-chat they had engaged in the night before. Their talk was about clothing, boyfriends, careers, which was all natural, but when they raised the question of conservation they prattled on about the natives who just did not know how to look after the land. Eleanor was careful not to air her opinions too strongly. As with Swanny, she needed to avoid any form of sharp disagreement that might fuel suspicion. So she simply raised, as a thought, the fact that most of the land in Natal was used for sugarcane farming. Had that perhaps not created the biggest problem for the natural environment and the people?

The following day one of the young women announced that her boyfriend would soon be coming to visit from the Cape. He was training to be a policeman, she announced matter-of-factly. At the first opportunity Eleanor asked Hugh if he knew about this. It was news to him and she told him that the sooner she left, the better. He understood the urgency and was concerned about the palpable fear Eleanor showed. He said it would be difficult leaving his work at such short notice but he would get the other rangers to cover for him. If they left very early the next morning, at 3 am, he could get her to Johannesburg by noon and be back at the camp the same evening. Fearing roadblocks, they decided she would again disguise herself as a boy.

27

As Hugh had planned, they were duly on the road at three, cruising through the Zululand bush in the dead of night and reaching the main road to Johannesburg at a turnoff to the Transvaal highveld at 7 am. The traffic was soon building up with no sight of police or roadblocks. Eleanor became excited as they came to the outskirts of Johannesburg and she directed him to the densely stacked skyscrapers of Hillbrow. This cosmopolitan area was in proximity to the safe houses she had known. At her request he parked near a telephone booth as she made a call.

She looked quickly through a telephone directory and found the firm of architects she needed. She asked to speak to John Bizzell, her Durban friend and recruit into the underground. He had been taking care of Ronnie and was in touch with Bram Fischer.

She could sense his excitement when he spoke to her. He told her to get off the streets 'pronto'. He directed her to a safe house she and Ronnie had stayed in once before in nearby Parktown. 'Go there and wait. I'll be with you in twenty minutes,' he instructed.

She got Hugh to drop her around the corner from the address and walked quickly to her destination. It was a large double-storey mansion with a small cottage at the rear. There was no sign of life anywhere. She hung about, at first at the front door of the cottage, and then at the back, where she felt less noticeable. She tried to peer through the windows but they were shut and the curtains were drawn. Though it appeared the place was empty, she thought she heard a faint sound from within. She listened more intently but there was silence and she thought she had imagined hearing something. Again there was a faint rustling. Was it a cat or dog? She moved back to the front door to listen. She was breathing hard. She sensed there was someone inside and decided to tap lightly on the door. 'Hello ... hello ... anyone home?' she whispered.

The door suddenly opened a little. Her heart leapt for joy as she recognised Ronnie. He was startled, however, at the sight of a frail-looking boy, with dark hair, wearing grey trousers and a school jacket. As recognition dawned, he pulled her into the room. They hugged and embraced, and were laughing for sheer joy. 'Oh my dear,' he cried, 'you're free and safe!' They whirled about the room in a dance of sheer ecstasy, kissing and hugging as though they had just won a fortune. They fell on the bed in passionate excitement. She had to contain his exuberance. 'Wait, John will be here any minute.'

He lit a cigarette for her and then one for himself, his hands trembling with the excitement of her surprise arrival. She began to outline her story from the time of her arrest and the treatment by Grobler, which she had written about in part in her letter to him. As she filled in the details of Grobler's abusive behaviour, he seethed with anger. 'I could kill him,' he muttered.

At that point John Bizzell arrived, tremendously elated to see Eleanor safe and sound. 'How did you do it? Fantastic!

Wonderful! Amazing! You, Eleanor, even in nursery school, as shy as you were, have always been a surprise package. You remember at Treetops what you did when I put a caterpillar down your back?'

'Yes, I do,' she answered, smiling mischievously. 'I put jelly down yours. And I thought I was so smart getting the girls to call you Jellybelly.'

They were both keen to hear Eleanor's full story, so she commenced from the time of her arrest for John's benefit. She told them everything, in a quiet, modest way, without seeking approval or acclaim, without a shred of overstatement, as though anyone could have pulled off the deception and organised the escape as she had. The only time she cared to dramatise was demonstrating how the African cleaner, herself a mental patient, would whip cigarettes from the unsuspecting hand or mouth of an inmate. Eleanor took a quiet pleasure in the re-enactment and in the surprise on the faces of her enraptured audience as she deftly relieved them of their smokes.

After celebrating with lunch and chilled white wine, John left for work and that evening returned with Bram Fischer.

28

The avuncular, silver-haired man hugged her warmly and spoke to her in his kindly manner, delighted by her escape. He reiterated its importance to the morale of the Movement. He spent over an hour listening intently to every aspect of Eleanor's story – her experience in detention, the information she could provide about Bruno's collaboration (which he regarded as important in preparing the legal defence for the Rivonia men) – and was utterly engrossed by the way she had planned and executed her escape.

He only regretted that the country had to lose people like her and Ronnie. With the security crackdown, the situation had become extremely difficult. Just to get the Goldreich escapees out safely had been a major undertaking. With the forthcoming Rivonia trial, due to start in October, and clearly Billy Nair's and Curnick Ndlovu's trial in Natal, above-ground people like John Bizzell, Pedro and Rob were rare and overstretched. It was increasingly difficult to cater for those on the run, especially the whites, because their support base was so small. African, Indian and Coloured comrades had the backing of the vast majority of people and could more easily be absorbed. Not only was it extremely dangerous and difficult to look after Eleanor and Ronnie for a prolonged period but it would be a huge setback if they fell into the hands of the SB.

Arrangements were being made to get the two of them across the border to safety. They would be leaving within a week. John would take them to another safe house when the time was ready, where they would be given disguises and documents. Bram would next see them there. They would join the exile structures and be trained abroad. Ronnie would go for military training while Eleanor was a natural underground operative because she was so unobtrusive and showed an evident knack for it. She would get special training in clandestine work and herself train others.

He told them that Joe Slovo had been sent abroad to attend to just those kinds of requirements. The Movement would recover, hopefully in the short term. He believed that immense pressure was building up against the apartheid government from abroad, even from the Americans. The mass struggle would resume and those being trained abroad would return. The situation was not hopeless.

Regarding the emphasis the Durban Security Branch had placed on whether Ronnie was Jewish, he agreed that the government was obsessive about a Jewish conspiracy. The 'Goldreich–Slovo clan' was a term that the SB's top theoretician, Major Coetzee, was actually peddling. Victims of their own propaganda, they thought it could be used to impress the West, given the residue of anti-semitism that existed in the world and the one-time connection of Jewish communists with Bolshevik Russia. But it was laughable. Clearly to show that the apartheid government was not anti-semitic, they were appointing Percy Yutar, a conservative Jew, to prosecute Mandela and the others.

Eleanor had often spoken to Bram about Brigid. He had

Eleanor and Brigid on Durban beach in 1962.

given her advice. At least she was safe for the time being with Eleanor's parents. As her ex-husband had hardly bothered with his daughter since their separation, Bram pointed out that it would become more difficult for him to prevent her parents from sending the child to her, if they were so inclined, once she was safe. Eleanor would obviously need to remain outside the country and set up a home if she was going to bring up her child. She could still be of use to the Movement but he was cautious, not wanting her to think that reuniting with Brigid would be easy. So much would depend on the willingness of her parents to co-operate.

There was no hope of going to fetch Brigid to take her with them. She and Ronnie had discussed this. Though he and John Bizzell were up for it, she had balked at the thought of whisking the child off the streets. They would have had to intercept her on her way to or from school. And she was always taken and fetched by her mother's domestic worker. In all probability the Special Branch would be closely watching her parents and even Brigid. They were well aware that Eleanor had been longing for her. It was all too dangerous, too risky to think of going near Durban. To request help for such an undertaking would, she saw, be unfair on Bram and the underground network, overwhelmed as they were with other pressing matters, including the coming Rivonia trial. So she suspended her longing and tried to swallow the pain.

29

They soon received word from John that the time for departure had come. They had been told they would be disguised as a Muslim couple. Eleanor would have her appearance altered by an expert at the next stop, while Ronnie had already been growing a moustache and beard.

'What about a bit of cross-dressing?' she had joked. 'You go as the Muslim lady and me as the *molvi* [priest]. Would you like that?'

She cut his hair very short and dyed it black like hers. She instructed John to purchase a dark suit, a Muslim-style shirt with no collar from an Asiatic bazaar and a *topi* (prayer cap). Ronnie already had a pair of heavy-rimmed spectacles with plain glass.

They eyed him critically in his full attire, cap in place, and agreed that with his dark complexion, and in the right company, he could easily pass muster as a Muslim. 'After all, Jews and Muslims are cousins,' they quipped.

John drove them to Fordsburg, an Indian quarter close to the city centre, and they slipped into a first-floor flat. The building was filled with life. Families were sitting down to the evening meal; Indian music blared out; and the tantalising smell of Eastern spice and incense perfumed the air.

A woman called Fatima* welcomed them. She had been expecting three white comrades and was momentarily unsure of the mysterious Muslim man. She looked Ronnie up and down, remarked that he seemed like an Indian merchant and presumed he was the comrade leaving with Eleanor. She promised that once they had eaten, she would transform Eleanor into an 'acceptable *slamse vrou* [Islamic wife]' for him.

Having invited them to sit down, she served a meal of curried chicken, pilau rice, minced meat with a yogurt dressing, salad and papadum, accompanied by refreshing cold mint tea. John suggested that Eleanor and Ronnie eat as much curry as possible to make the aroma pervade their very being. 'Just let a cop get a smell of you and he won't need to be convinced that you're 100 per cent *charras* [Indians].'

Fatima did not want to rush them, but as soon as they had eaten she remarked that Eleanor's disguise would take some time and they needed to start the preparation. The two women went into a dressing room while John and Ronnie continued eating with gusto.

Fatima had laid out some beautiful Punjabi clothing: white cotton pantaloon trousers and a purple and mauve overdress, which hung to Eleanor's knees. It was studded with sequins and had a high collar, which suited her elegant neckline. Appropriate costume jewellery, drop earrings and bracelets were added for the effect. 'You look simply regal,' she told Eleanor.

'Fit for a sheikh, am I?' Eleanor responded girlishly and Fatima laughed.

* Fatima Adams, sister-in-law of Babla Saloojee.

'Next,' she announced, 'we'll darken your eyebrows, and apply kohl to your eyelashes and under your eyes, so as to make you a perfect Islamic beauty.' The blue in Eleanor's light grey eyes seemed more pronounced after the expert application of the cosmetic.

'Now for the crowning glory,' Fatima announced proudly, producing a magnificent black wig. Eleanor eagerly tried it on and with Fatima's assistance pulled it expertly into place. The hair hung down to her shoulders and Fatima brushed it so that it hung loose and natural. Eleanor looked critically at herself in the mirror, from various angles. Stepping back to get a good look at the full-length effect, she liked what she saw. 'I'm a bit pale for a good Muslim,' she remarked.

'Nowhere near as pale as my aunties from Kashmir,' Fatima exclaimed. 'But yes, we're going to make you darker, and I've already mixed the colouring.'

She produced a jar of brown cream and asked Eleanor to remove the wig. She began to apply the mixture to Eleanor's face, neck and hands. 'Does it feel too sticky? Is it comfortable enough?' she enquired.

'I can live with it,' was the reply. 'What is it?'

'Basic foundation cream, mixed with a teeny bit of coffee powder. Is it too strong?'

Eleanor joked about 'smelling like an Italian cappuccino'. Fatima told her not to worry; they would cover the aroma with perfume. With the wig in place, Eleanor went back into the parlour to see what Ronnie and John thought.

They enthusiastically applauded her entrance as Fatima proclaimed: 'Curry to repel the police; coffee-cream to attract an Italian; an attire to seduce a maharaja; perfume to knock

130

the socks off any remaining male!' Fatima wagged a finger at Ronnie: 'And you make the perfect partner. But mind, only one wife, hey!'

Before long Bram Fischer arrived, as courteous and unruffled as ever. He was impressed with their appearance and sat down at a table with the two of them, producing letters and cards which identified them as Enver and Farida Sulimann, a newly married couple who would be travelling to visit relatives near the Bechuanaland border. He told them that they would be accompanied by two Indian comrades who were adept at ferrying people to border crossing points. They would be in safe, experienced hands. There would be an old man joining them shortly, Julius First, who was Ruth First's father. He, too, was on the run but was none too well. They would need to take care of him. 'He's a bit grouchy, but don't let that get you down.' There would be comrades waiting on the other side of the border fence, who would take over and arrange for their onward journey to Dar es Salaam. He gave them a few hundred rands to tide them over any difficulties.

They were to give the leadership in Dar es Salaam a full report about what had happened in Natal and inform them that the Rivonia trial would start within a few weeks. The government was planning to press ahead with all trials, especially the Rivonia trial, to pre-empt the building up of international pressure. Nelson Mandela, already serving a five-year sentence, had been brought from prison by the prosecution to join the leaders captured at Rivonia. The government would want heavy sentences, if not the death sentence, for all. Fischer's view, however, was that even though Britain and the United States did not want to see the death penalty imposed, it would be touch and go.

They soon met their driver, a bubbly young man in his thirties, who they came to learn was Babla Saloojee, Fatima's brother-in-law. He had made a name for himself as a daring and resourceful activist. He was a fast-talking, quick-witted, bouncing ball of energy who infected everyone with his sense of humour. He greeted them warmly, said that he had Julius First in his car and announced that they needed to get going. They climbed into the back of the Pontiac, with Eleanor seated between Ronnie and Julius. He turned out to be a taciturn old man dressed in a suit and *topi* like Ronnie, who smoked a cigar oblivious of the fact that it filled the car with pungent fumes. He was fleeing the country because of his connection with the purchase of the Rivonia property. He scarcely responded to Eleanor and Ronnie's polite greeting. In the passenger seat was another elderly gentleman, Molvi Cachalia, whose long beard and traditional Muslim garb gave him the appearance of a priest. He touched his heart, nodded politely and said '*Salaam alakum*' to them. When they responded '*Alakum salaam*' he was pleased and said it was an auspicious start, for they were behaving like authentic Muslims.

30

It was already late at night, as they travelled westwards on the Main Reef Road past the continuous belt of gold-mine dumps that lined the route. All the fugitives found it difficult to sit back and relax, and they peered constantly into the road ahead, imagining a police roadblock at every turn. Eleanor had lapsed into a deep silence and squeezed Ronnie's hand until her knuckles were white. Julius First lit up another cigar, which did not help Eleanor's mood and caused her to cough. She tried wafting the smoke away with her hands yet he paid no attention to her obvious discomfort. He sat tense and silent in his own impregnable shell and puffed away. Ronnie offered to change positions with Eleanor so that she could be more comfortable by the window. Overhearing this, Babla intervened and, addressing Mr First with great deference as 'Uncle Julius', asked him if he would please put out the cigar, indicating that they would stop in a couple of hours for what he called 'a body break'. Julius cast an irritated side-long glance at Eleanor, and noisily stubbed out his cigar in an ashtray, which succeeded in producing even more of a stench.

'Now, folks, don't worry about roadblocks,' Babla continued breezily, in an effort to cut through the tension building up in the rear seat. He explained that a pilot car had driven ahead earlier in the evening and had telephoned Johannesburg to report that the route was clear. The same car was again on the road, an hour ahead of them. If the driver came across any police check-point that had only recently been set up, he would have time to turn back and warn them.

'In any event,' he explained, 'if we do come across a roadblock, just leave Molvi and me to do the talking. We have a good story. Molvi is actually officiating at a wedding in the border region and we have the papers confirming it.'

They drove on through the night in what was a desolate part of the country, encountering little traffic, and flashed past occasional platteland dorps. At a lay-by they stretched their legs and drank coffee from a flask. When the pilot car arrived at the rendezvous point, Babla conferred with the driver. He served the man a mug of coffee and then the pilot car was off again, driving back the way he had come.

When they, too, were once more on the road, Babla explained that they were not far from Mafeking, the largest town near the Bechuanaland border. They would be stopping there briefly. The pilot car had reported that the route into town was absolutely clear.

They drove into Mafeking at an easy pace, not wanting to break the speed limit. The main street was lined with trading stores and a few colonial buildings that seemed to recall the famous Boer War siege over sixty years earlier. They stopped at an all-night garage to fill up with petrol. Babla kept the African attendant engaged in easy chit-chat and then paid the bill to a sleepy white man at the pay point who took only a cursory glance at their vehicle.

Well before dawn they pulled into a neat house in the Indian business sector of Mafeking for a short rest and some breakfast. It appeared to belong to the driver of the pilot vehicle. He greeted them while his wife served up rice and dhal, boiled eggs, samoosas, coffee and fresh fruit. He had a quiet word with Babla and then drove off again. Babla explained that they would follow him within ten minutes. His friend would continue to scout the road ahead.

They duly departed. Travelling due west of the town, they found themselves as dawn was breaking in open terrain, with scattered thorn tress, rocky outcrops and bush stretching to the horizon. Small bands of goats eyed them as they sped along a dirt road. There had been bursts of conversation in the car, but once they were well away from Mafeking silence descended. They began picking up speed. Babla explained that they were now in the northern Cape with Bechuanaland to the north and beyond that, he said with a grin, 'Mother Africa, the giantess, awakening from her slumbers'.

They encountered no other vehicles save for the occasional peasant on a bicycle, with a heavy load of blankets or wood on the back, and sedate donkey carts driven by wizened owners. The road began to veer towards the north and from time to time they got a glimpse of the border fence. They rode for several more miles with the road sometimes running abreast of the border, sometimes veering towards it and then away again. Babla told them they were nearing the crossing point and began slowing down in an area boasting a few green trees – the sign of a nearby stream. In fact the vegetation was growing by a dried-out river bed. A small village loomed into view, and he brought the vehicle to a halt, with the engine idling.

'This is it,' he announced. 'Move quickly now.' Eleanor and Ronnie needed no encouragement and unloaded the baggage, a light hold-all which they shared and two heavy bags belonging to Julius. Babla gave them swift directions, indicating a wooden ladder straddling the border fence a few hundred metres distant. 'That's the way over,' he explained. 'It's used by the locals whose village huts are on both sides of the border line drawn by the colonisers.'

He pointed out a red-roofed building on a ridge on the Bechuanaland side. 'That's where you must head. The building's a trading store. Comrades in a green Land Rover will be there to pick you up. Hamba kahle!'

Julius and Molvi were still deep in conversation, dragging out their farewells, when Eleanor called out in alarm that a vehicle was coming. They could see a fast-moving dust cloud approaching from the Mafeking direction. It appeared to be less than a mile away. With Eleanor supporting Julius, Ronnie picked up all three bags, and they struggled as best they could for cover. Meanwhile Babla and Molvi jumped into the car and sped off. Sheltering behind a screen of boulders, the trio watched in trepidation as a police vehicle sped by, seemingly in hot pursuit of Babla. They thanked their lucky stars that they had not been spotted.

As soon as the whine of its engine had died down, they were on the move, hoping that Babla and Molvi would be able to talk their way out of trouble. Although they only had a few hundred metres to cover before reaching the ladder, it proved more difficult than it looked. They laboured up a slope, the thorn trees tearing at their clothing, and picked their way through several *dongas*. It had become very warm, and the suits the two men wore became uncomfortable. Julius First was having trouble breathing and Eleanor's make-up

136

was running. At least she had shed the wig and Punjabi dress, giving them to Babla to return to Fatima. Her short urchin cut was a blessing, but she struggled to support Julius, who leant heavily on her. Ronnie literally had his hands full with the three bags and he, too, was soon panting for breath. At last they reached the ladder. There were homesteads nearby and some young boys, kicking a tennis ball about, stared at them in astonishment. One broke away and ran helter-skelter home, either to tell his parents or simply because he was terrified. They hoped that nobody would appear to challenge them at this final stage of their escape.

Eleanor was first up the ladder, which was handmade but firm and sturdy. The fence was over two metres high. She waited at the top to give Julius a hand as Ronnie supported him from behind, then guided him safely down. Because the bags were too big to be passed through the fence, Ronnie had to heft them up to the top of the ladder and pass them down to Eleanor one at a time. Finally he got over himself.

Although they were relieved to be on the soil of the British Protectorate of Bechuanaland, they were still far from being at ease. White farmers lived along the border and could pose a danger. Fortunately, as if scripted in a movie, they spotted a dark green Land Rover, silhouetted against the northern skyline, coming to a halt at the store with the red roof. Its arrival could not have been more perfectly timed.

31

By the time they reached the store Eleanor's face was a sticky mess, Julius First was having palpitations and Ronnie's arms were so seized with cramp that he could not straighten them. Their reception party consisted of two comrades who assisted them into the Land Rover. They gratefully accepted a water bottle to slake their thirst. As they drove off for the southern town of Lobatse, the relief coursing through their bodies, Eleanor began giggling like a little girl at the sight of Ronnie trying to stretch his arms. He, too, began guffawing at the sight of her runny make-up and the smile lines on her brow and around her eyes, which were white. His chuckles prompted greater mirth on her side. 'Oh stop it, stop it!' she pleaded, the tears running down her cheeks, but this simply made matters worse. It was the equivalent of their dancing wildly around the Parktown cottage when she had arrived after escaping from Fort Napier. No sooner had a bout of laughter died down than their bodies were engulfed in yet another wave of mirth, until they became utterly, happily exhausted. Normally shy of exhibiting themselves in front of even close friends, they hugged one another tightly, begged the comrades to excuse their insanity, and even ignored Julius First, whose manner of celebrating was to light up one of his cigars.

The driver of the Land Rover was Fish Keitseng, a

Bechuanaland citizen, who had been a member of the ANC in South Africa. He and his companion were part of the underground pipeline established by the ANC. They drove to his home in the township outside Lobatse and were carried into the modest dwelling wrapped in blankets. It was explained that vigilance was necessary as apartheid's secret agents were very active in the territory. The previous month a charter plane for ANC fugitives, including Goldreich and Wolpe, had been blown up in the dead of night.

Having arrived in Bechuanaland, they would have to report their arrival in person to the District Commissioner. Arrangements would then be made to fly them quietly off to Tanganyika. Fish Keitseng had received a coded message to say that Babla and Molvi were fine. It was a huge relief. The police had stopped them but accepted their story. Eleanor remarked how considerate Babla was, 'taking the trouble to let us know, since he knew we would be worried'.

After cleaning up and a short rest they were taken to the District Commissioner's office in Lobatse and got their first glimpse of the Union Jack flying from a tall flagpole. The Victorian architecture reminded Eleanor of Fort Napier. The premises were guarded by black policemen with rifles – something South Africans were not used to. As a foretaste of the Commissioner's character, a messenger arrived from his office with mail in a forked stick and clapped his hands to gain admission. The Commissioner was an arrogant man, clad in colonial-style shorts and shirt. He looked snootily at this latest trio of refugees fleeing South Africa because they were probably communists. He sneered at Julius First for having to flee his country at his age.

'With all due respect, Mr Commissioner,' Eleanor cut in, 'I don't see what business that is of yours.' The Commissioner blanched and snapped back, saying that he would not countenance being interrupted. She rolled her eyes at the ceiling in clear contempt of the man. Ignoring her, he questioned them on the route they had used to enter Her Majesty's territory. Fish Keitseng had advised them, for security reasons, to give a different route from the one they had used. They replied that they had jumped the fence to the east of Lobatse. He then asked which way they'd turned once they reached the tarred road. 'Left,' said Eleanor and simultaneously Ronnie uttered, 'Right.' Neither could conceal their mirth and the Commissioner went scarlet with rage. He told them they were impertinent and that the sooner they left his territory the better. He turned to one of his assistants and told him to issue the necessary documentation. They were granted leave to stay in Bechuanaland until they could obtain transport out of the country and were given two weeks to do so.

Now that they were officially in Bechuanaland, Fish Keitseng suggested they book into a local hotel under assumed names and announce they were tourists. Staying in the township would draw unwanted attention. So they checked into a white-washed double-storey hotel which looked as though Baden-Powell might have used it during the Boer War. It had a corrugated roof and a spacious balcony running along its front. They gave their name as Grobler, to irritate the Durban Special Branch policeman who in time would trace their movements. Julius posed as Ronnie's father. They explained that while touring the territory their vehicle had

140

broken down. It was undergoing extensive repairs and they simply wanted to enjoy a quiet rest for several days. The hotel manager took them at face value and confided that the town was no longer as quiet as it once had been, with all manner of terrorists fleeing South Africa. He let them know that two months before, the notorious communists Jack and Rica Hodgson had come that way and actually stayed in the hotel, having jumped house-arrest orders in Johannesburg.

They were allocated a suite of rooms with an adjoining sitting room where they spent a nerve-racking fortnight waiting for a charter flight to be arranged. They passed the time doing jigsaw puzzles and playing cards. Ronnie tried valiantly to maintain the peace between Eleanor and Julius, but the old man continued to irritate her by smoking his cigars indoors. She could hardly complain, seeing that she was fast on the way to becoming a chain-smoker herself. At any rate the new field of battle centred on the game table. Julius took ages playing his hand at poker or rummy as though his life depended on it. While Eleanor enjoyed playing patience, which she breezed through, round upon round, with speed and dexterity, Julius would hover over her, puffing his cigar and interfering with her selection. 'Mr First, please do me a favour,' she coldly declared. 'Patience is an individual game; that's why the Americans call it solitaire.'

The poor man did not have good enough eyesight to help with the jigsaw puzzle. They had bought one with 10 000 pieces and would pass hours of time meticulously building up the picture of an English manor house with rose garden. When they were not at the table, Julius would fuss over the pieces. Returning to the table for a session, Eleanor discovered several misplaced pieces and remonstrated with him: 'Mr First, would you kindly stop rummaging around with these pieces,' she cried. 'You'll end up losing some.'

Ronnie sprang to his defence. 'Come on, Eleanor, don't take things so seriously.'

'Oh really?' she screamed at him. 'Take his damn side. See if I care. Finish the jigsaw yourself!' and she stormed into their bedroom in tears.

He followed her while Julius began fiddling with the puzzle, apparently unconcerned.

She was on their bed blowing her nose and looking utterly miserable. Before he could speak she was at him. 'You've done nothing about his damn cigar smoke: the sitting room is filthy with ash. He never has a civil word to say to me. I want to strangle him when he interferes with my cards. And you don't say a word to him.' She began to sob.

'Look,' he pleaded, 'he's an old man. He's left his wife and family behind. He must be feeling terrible. Bram asked us to take care of him, didn't he?'

'Take care of him? That doesn't mean he can treat me as if I don't exist.'

They were getting nowhere. She picked up a book to read and turned her back on him. That evening at dinner she clammed up and would not speak to him at all, although she made a point of being very civil to Julius.

The last straw was when they all went shopping the next day. While they were in a general dealer's store, the Indian owner remarked confidentially to the two of them that Julius should not let on that they were refugees from the south. They were taken aback and enquired what exactly he meant. 'Well,'

142

the shopkeeper explained, 'he was asking what discount I would give and I told him 10 per cent. He then put in a plea as a "refugee from South Africa" for something a bit more generous. But you see, this is not wise; these are dangerous times. You can't trust anyone, black or white.'

Eleanor exploded. She immediately stormed out of the shop, snapping at Ronnie: 'That's it! I know he is an old man who has left his wife and family behind, but his actions are placing us all in jeopardy. Looking after him, as Bram requested, means protecting him from his own miserliness, and I expect you to deal with him.' With that she strode back to the hotel. It was left to Ronnie to accompany Julius back from the store and say a quiet word to him on the way.

On the day of their departure the Johannesburg *Sunday Times* carried a photograph of Julius First and a report that he had disappeared and was wanted by the police for his role in the purchase of the Rivonia property. They were relieved to have checked out of the hotel already. 'Imagine how the tongues will be wagging. And wait until Grobler hears we used his name. I bet that'll raise his blood pressure,' Ronnie commented.

They finally took off in a small six-seater aircraft for Tanganyika, which had recently attained independence. Just prior to departure they were declared prohibited immigrants by the Commissioner's office, the official papers being served on them at the small airstrip. Two other ANC members joined them for the trip.

Their pilot was a garrulous Afrikaner who sounded somewhat sinister. Within five minutes of being airborne he bragged that he had engaged in gun-running for Tshombe in

Katanga, and claimed to be one of the few gentiles who, for a reason he failed to disclose, had his name in Israel's 'Golden Book of the Jews'. Ronnie sat behind him with a hunting knife, his eyes glued to the compass needle, while Eleanor was feeling none too well from the fumes of Julius First's cigars.

They landed at Kasane on the banks of the Zambezi River in the remote north-eastern part of Bechuanaland, after the pilot had swept over great herds of elephant grazing and bathing in the swamps. The District Commissioner at Kasane was even more hostile than the one at Lobatse and, after informing them that he could not guarantee their safety overnight, petulantly insisted that they sleep in the local jail. He then stalked off in his pith helmet and shorts, with a dog at his heels, reminding Eleanor and Ronnie of the near-sighted Mr Magoo, for he was a diminutive, grumpy old man with thick-lensed spectacles. While the pilot spent the night in the local hotel, they were taken by very considerate Batswana policemen to the cells. Driving past the hotel they noticed a Volkswagen in the parking lot. It gave them the jitters, given their experience of the Durban Special Branch's preference for that model. It had a South African registration plate and Eleanor remarked suspiciously, 'That's a long way from home.' They hoped it just belonged to some innocent tourist.

They had arranged with the pilot to send them cold drinks. A hotel waiter duly arrived with opened bottles of Coca-Cola. The police constable was suspicious and advised them to send the bottles back, saying that something might have been added. In his view the local whites were not to be trusted and news of their recent arrival was circulating. They were of course quite aware that their pilot would be regaling one

144

and all at the hotel bar with stories of the latest communist fugitives he was transporting to Tanganyika. They wondered with a little trepidation what the owner of the Volkswagen might be thinking. That night, while Julius First and Eleanor slept, Ronnie and the two ANC comrades took turns keeping watch from the doorway of the police station.

The following day they flew over Zambia and landed at Mbaye in Tanganyika. It was lush and green and, with its atmosphere of peace and distance from South Africa, they at last felt free and able to relax. They stayed the night in a small hotel, thrilled to be in an independent African state. After meeting a Russian, who turned out to be from the Soviet trade mission, they went to the local cinema and saw a *Carry On* film with Syd James and Barbara Windsor, just the sort of silly escapist comedy their frayed nerves required. Once the double entendre gags started flowing about Barbara Windsor's 'headlights' and other English lavatory humour, they were convulsed with laughter again, as they had been in Fish Keitseng's Land Rover. Clearly the film was doing them a load of good. They wondered, though, what the Swahili-speaking audience would make of the film's gags and of their own hysterical mirth.

At the end of the film the audience stood to attention as a recording of the Tanganyikan national anthem was played against the backdrop of the black, green and gold colours of the country's flag. The tune and the colours were based on those of the ANC, the first African national movement in the continent. They felt extremely proud. It seemed to draw a line under the most dramatic period in their young and eventful lives. Their involvement in the liberation struggle, which had occupied a mere three years, seemed like a lifetime. It was exactly sixty days from Eleanor's arrest on 19 August to their safe arrival in Tanganyika. She whispered to him that her Odyssey was not yet over. To his question what she meant by that, she answered wistfully: 'Well, Brigid is still in Durban, isn't she?'

32

They arrived in Dar es Salaam – Arabic for 'Haven of Peace' – the following day to a boisterous reception from the ANC and met top leaders like Moses Kotane, J.B. Marks and Duma Nokwe, who were struggle icons. Eleanor received a bouquet of flowers from her friend, Maud Manyosi, leader of a nurses' strike at King George V Hospital in Durban, who was now working in the ANC office. She was one of the growing number of members either being deployed in exile or going further afield for military training or to study in the professions. Eleanor had befriended her in Durban after organising solidarity support for the striking nurses.

The ANC was housed in a shabby ground-floor office in a dilapidated building on the newly named Independence Avenue. The two gave a verbal report about the situation at home, covering the Durban detentions and Eleanor's escape as well as the messages from Bram Fischer. The leadership said Eleanor's escape story was so dramatic that it would be a good thing to have a press conference. Would she be agreeable? Though a bit nervous about the suggestion, she agreed.

They went and chatted to ANC staff. Maud worked there and so did Mosie Moola and Abdulhay Jassat, who had escaped with Goldreich and Wolpe from detention over two months before. Mosie was a lively individual with a flashing

smile. Eleanor was tickled pink when she discovered that the disguise Mosie had used when he fled South Africa was the self-same Punjabi attire and wig she had worn. Abdulhay had been subjected to electric shock torture while in detention and was suffering from epileptic attacks.

Over the next few days the newcomers were shown around Dar es Salaam and drank in the exotic atmosphere with its mix of Africa and the East. It was a most beautiful city with extremely friendly people, who greeted them with the Swahili *jumbo* (hello) and *karibu* (welcome). Dhows from the Persian Gulf sailed into the harbour, along with modern vessels and local fishing boats. The Gulf Arabs would roll out their carpets on the pavements, together with other exotic wares, sit on their haunches all day long, and engage in vigorous bargaining. Swahili vendors along the harbour wall sold sweet potato with a chilli powder dressing, tropical fruit and barbecued meat

on spits. Tall, lithe Masai warriors from the interior in ochre cloaks traded their artefacts.

They came to enjoy sitting on the terrace of the New Africa Hotel, a splendid colonial building – all wood and white paint, palm trees and verandas – which was a meeting place for diplomats, politicians, freedom fighters and spies. Dar es Salaam was on the crossroads of the various liberation movements, including those from Angola, Mozambique, Namibia and Zimbabwe as well as South Africa. They had in fact been warned to be on the alert and to be careful what they said to strangers, including friends purportedly sympathetic to the ANC. They sipped cold beers and snacked on cashew nuts. They learnt to call out to the waiters in red fezzes: 'Tusker beer, *baridi sana, bwana*' (very cold, mister) and acknowledged the prompt service with the polite expression *asanti sane* (thank you very much).

And then a glitch occurred: they perceived a coolness developing towards them. At first they thought they were imagining things and desperately hoped that nothing untoward would develop – not after all the trials and tribulations they had been through. A message then arrived from the ANC office to tell them to take things easy. This was welcome. However, each morning an ANC car would arrive at their hotel to fetch Julius First while they seemed to be forgotten. For his part, Julius ignored them completely. One day they chanced upon him checking out at reception with his luggage and realised he was departing. Ronnie had a word with the ANC driver, who told him that the old man was on his way to London. Julius walked straight past them without so much as a farewell.

The following day Maud arrived to tell them that Mr First had been bad-mouthing the two of them, especially Eleanor, whom he described as 'no good'. But Duma Nokwe had instructed her to tell them not to worry: the ANC was expecting a report from Bram Fischer and was sure it would clear things up. All the same, who were they, relative newcomers and unknown to most of the ANC leadership in Dar es Salaam, compared with an old communist like Julius First? It was a bitter pill to swallow, even allowing for Julius's advanced age and pitiful circumstances[*].

They cheered each other up by exploring the city, its museums and market places, and swimming in its warm bays. At last they were called to the ANC office and discovered that everything was back to normal. They were in from the cold and once more part of the family.

* Later in London they reconciled with him.

Eleanor at Zaheer Guest House.

The ANC leadership informed them that while their further training was being considered, they would remain in Dar es Salaam for several months because training programmes would only commence the following year. In the meantime they would help out in the ANC office, in the publication section with Mosie Moola, and they would be transferred to a guest house nearby where some of the office workers stayed. They would be taken the following morning to the Department of Home Affairs to register as refugees and as ANC workers. But first there would be a press conference for Eleanor because news of her escape from police custody, and safe arrival in Dar es Salaam, was very positive for the ANC.

Eleanor found the press conference harrowing, having qualms about recounting details of her ordeal at the hands of the apartheid Security Police in public. She smoked continuously throughout and answered the questions as best she could. In fact she did very well. The *Tanganyika Standard* gave the story front-page coverage under the banner headline 'REFUGEE TELLS OF STARVATION: WOMAN FLEES TO DAR AFTER ESCAPE FROM S.A. ASYLUM.'

Alongside a photograph of a slender and wan-looking Eleanor, cigarette in her long fingers, the story ran: 'A young woman who was sent to a mental hospital six days after she had been detained by the South African security police; who was put in jail in solitary confinement under the 90-day detention law; who went on starvation strike because of the "injustice" of her arrest, and who escaped from the closely-guarded asylum, yesterday told the *Tanganyika Standard* her story.'

For Eleanor it was a relief to have got over the interview. That evening she and Ronnie transferred to the Zaheer Guest House, off Mosque Street, in the Asian quarter of the city. It was a three-storey building, with large, sparsely furnished rooms, mosquito netting on the beds, electric fans on the ceiling, windows with good views of the street, communal bathrooms and what was referred to as 'Asiatic toilets' where one squatted instead of sitting. They were delighted to find that Mosie and Abdulhay shared a room next to theirs. That evening they ate dinner at the Zaheer restaurant, which served hot curried mutton, chicken or minute shrimps with rice. As no alcohol was allowed on the premises, they later walked in the warm evening air down to the harbour and drank cold beer in celebration of their new life.

33

The next day an ANC liaison officer took them to register at Home Affairs. They were soon seated in an office with two civil servants. One of them had a questionnaire and opted, with a pleasant smile, to take 'Mama first'.

He asked her full name, date and place of birth, name of father and mother, and so on.

'What's your tribe?' was the next question.

'Tribe?' she said. 'I don't have a tribe.'

'Everyone must have a tribe, Mama.'

'Oh, well what about White South African?'

He shook his head.

'European?' she volunteered.

'No, that's too general.'

'I was born in Scotland, so will Scots do?'

'Ah, now that's right. A fine tribe, the Scots.'

'Now, let's turn to your father. Born in Scotland you say, but living and working in South Africa now?'

To this she readily agreed.

'What is his occupation?'

'He is an agent.'

A quizzical note crept into his voice: 'An agent – an agent for whom?'

'He is an agent for Arwa.'

'Arwa? Who are Arwa?'

'They're a German company.'

'You mean your father's an agent for a German company? Tell me, how is it that your father, a Scotsman, living in South Africa, is an agent for the Germans?'

Both she and Ronnie tensed up, realising that she had been conveying the wrong impression. The fact that the other Home Affairs official, who had sat back simply to witness proceedings, pulled his chair closer and leant stiffly forward, did not help.

She took a deep breath and smiled demurely. 'Oh dear, what I am trying to tell you is that the term "agent" is common in South Africa for a representative of a business, and my father represents a German firm exporting Arwa stockings to South Africa – ladies' stockings.'

They looked on with raised eyebrows, the penny slowly dropping.

She continued: 'It's like any company from Germany, selling Mercedes-Benz cars in this country. You would call the salesman an agent for *Wabenzi*.'

They exploded with laughter, perhaps because her use of the term *Wabenzi* showed that she was already imbibing their Swahili phrases. *Wabenzi* was a reference to the new political-business elite and was used rather cynically by the common people and by lower-level civil servants like them.

After the questionnaire was filled out, she had to sit against a wall for the official photograph. She sat straight-backed and noticed that Ronnie was still chuckling quietly over her father being a 'German agent'. She struggled to keep a straight face, but to no avail. The photographer shook his head and said,

'Mama, this is for your registration card. Please don't smile.'

When they picked up their documents the next day, the official presented her with an additional envelope. 'That's the lovely picture of you with your pretty smile. Keep it as a souvenir.'

It turned out to be a most enchanting picture of her. She looks confidently at the camera with her warm, large eyes, full of life. Her hair is cut short and dyed black, and a scarf tied above her forehead speaks of good taste. A mischievous smile plays on her lips, which are full and sensual and reflect a human being with an irreverent sense of humour. She is slightly built, refined and demure, her looks belying an extraordinary mental toughness. Who could have guessed that this young woman had been engaged in sabotage operations, been brutally interrogated, engaged in a hunger strike, wheedled her way into a mental asylum from which she made a dramatic escape, and triumphed over the ruthless security police, an officer of which had threatened to 'break her or hang her' when she had been arrested a mere three months previously?

Ronnie fell in love with the photograph and immediately put it into his pocket book. 'I'm keeping that with me as long as I live.'

34

They saw in the new year, 1964, at midnight from their favourite spot on the harbour wall. They had been quietly walking hand in hand in the evening after a stiflingly humid day. As the most eventful year of their young lives drew to a close, she had grown tense, thinking of home and the daughter who remained behind. The harbour, the palm trees, the clammy heat at the height of summer, reminded them of Durban, 3000 kilometres south. When the ships in the harbour sounded their foghorns to welcome in the New Year – as would be happening that very moment in Durban – she longed for her daughter. She imagined Brigid listening to similar sounds from her parents' home on the Berea heights above the harbour. She laid her head on Ronnie's shoulder, clung to him, and cried pitifully. She feared she would never see Brigid again. The absence of her child over the festive period had been weighing heavily on her. She had tried to suppress the pangs of separation, stoically and silently, and had not wanted to inflict this on Ronnie, who had received the news from home that his father, aged only 63, had died of a sudden illness earlier that month.

They sat on the harbour wall, hugging one another, as the foghorns and sounds of revelry in the streets mocked their sadness. He cursed himself for failing to see the melancholy

*Ronnie with Ebrahim Desai, Mosie Moola and Abdulhay Jassat in
Dar es Salaam. Photo by Eleanor*

mood creeping up on her all day. He tried to console her.
Like so many others, she had responded to the injustice of
apartheid and the pressing needs of the struggle and, for the
sake of convenience and for reasons of security, had left her
daughter in the care of her parents.

She listened carefully but expressed the fear that her ex-
husband would never allow her child to leave the country. She
regretted not having gone back to Durban to fetch Brigid and
smuggle her out with them. He reminded her that this had
been discussed over and over with Bram Fischer and had been
rejected as too risky. He tried to cheer her up by reminding her
that Brigid was at least safe and well with her parents and that
surely they would help to convince her ex-husband when the
time came. When she pointed out that it was difficult to predict

how her parents would react when the things she and Ronnie had done were revealed in the coming trials – though most certainly her ex-husband would be extremely hostile – Ronnie tried another tack and assured her that the apartheid system would soon crack, as everyone in the Movement anticipated. She, however, was beginning to realise that it might take years and years, and that perhaps they would never get back home.

In the event, 1964 was not an easier year for them, for they were separated for over nine months when Ronnie was sent to the Soviet Union for military training. Eleanor postponed going on a separate training course until later, opting to work full-time in the ANC office in Dar es Salaam. She felt she could not afford to lose contact with her parents for any length of time. She wrote to them and Brigid and received letters and birthday cards in return. When someone she knew visited Dar es Salaam on a cruise liner which was calling at Durban, she was able to send Brigid a parcel of gifts, consisting of Swahili curios and toys. A letter from her mother, sounding cold and brusque, commented on the trial taking place in Pietermaritzburg of Billy Nair and company. 'Ronnie is damn lucky he was not caught. It would have been the rope for him!' she wrote. Eleanor felt it sounded as though she was virtually saying 'and he would have deserved it too!'

Her mother made it plain that there was no way they would be prepared to send Brigid to an African state. 'Eleanor, if you want to see your daughter, you'd better get to Britain. Go stay with your aunt in Scotland.' This hit Eleanor hard. It was not a case of her former husband not countenancing Brigid joining her in an African state but rather that they, her parents, would not be prepared to let her go. As far as Eleanor was concerned,

An ANC protest in Dar es Salaam with Mosie Moola (second left) and Maud Manyosi (second right). Photo by Eleanor

her ex-husband had no genuine interest in Brigid and was putty in her mother's hands. Confiding in Maud Manyosi, she said how much better it would in fact be for Brigid to grow up in independent Tanganyika rather than in racist South Africa.

It was tough without Ronnie, who was completely out of touch in the Soviet Union, but she conscientiously applied herself to her work in the ANC office, gaining the admiration of leadership and staff alike. Both Oliver Tambo, who arrived from London to take up office in Dar es Salaam, and Moses Kotane valued the personal assistance she gave them. Kotane, the ANC Treasurer, who trusted nobody but himself with the funds, soon had her driving him to the bank and on other errands. He ultimately gave her the responsibility of depositing and drawing money from the bank on his behalf. When it was decided to give the ANC office a face-lift, Tambo

160

found her most helpful with practical and creative ideas for redecoration.

She became particularly close to Mosie and Abdulhay and regularly attended the Indian cinema with them, enjoying the melodramas and musicals from the subcontinent. The community in the Asian quarter of Zaheer Guest House and Mosque Street virtually made her their ward, and she could walk the streets alone and unmolested, at whatever time of day or night. She was popular with the MK comrades who would come to the office from the transit camps to see one leader or another, and converse with her and Maud about their problems. Her closest friends amongst the leaders were J.B. Marks and Duma Nokwe. Sometimes after work she would sit with them on the balcony of their flat opposite the ANC office, drinking tea and laughing at their anecdotes about struggle times back home. Duma, who had been South Africa's first black advocate, listened to her story about Brigid and was of the view that she try the option of going to Britain. She befriended another white refugee from Johannesburg, Pam Beira, who had known Ronnie during their schooldays in Johannesburg. Pam had become attached to Marcelino dos Santos, one of the Frelimo leaders, and Eleanor became friendly with them and their group, including a young Joachim Chissano, future President of a liberated Mozambique. She grew to love Dar es Salaam and its people, and began speaking a passable Swahili.

35

It was October 1964, almost a year to the day that she and Ronnie had arrived in what had now become Tanzania. She heard on the ANC grapevine – 'Radio Potato' – that he was back from training and was in one of the transit camps on the outskirts of Dar es Salaam. When she asked Duma Nokwe whether she would have a chance to see Ronnie, he told her he would do something about it. First thing the following morning she heard Ronnie's familiar voice on the office telephone. He told her he had risked sneaking out of the camp to make the call and to tell her he was back. 'We simply must see each other!'

'Don't worry,' she told him. 'I had heard of your return. I requested seeing you and it is being arranged.'

They were soon together again. He was given twelve hours to be with her. They quite simply accepted the ANC's regulations and were only too grateful to be together once more, no matter how briefly.

They sat at their favourite spot at Banda beach, by the harbour mouth, where the dhows and ocean liners glided in. The dye in her hair had long grown out and it was naturally fair again. Her limpid grey eyes took on a light-blue sparkle in the sunlight as she informed him about the news he might have missed. In the Pietermaritzburg trial, Billy Nair and

Curnick Ndlovu had received 20-year sentences and Ebrahim Ismail Ebrahim 15 years. All the accused were in high spirits during the trial and had cheered when, in answer to a question about the case against Ronnie and Eleanor, information was given that she had escaped from Fort Napier and the two were in Tanzania with the ANC. The main state witness was Bruno Mtolo, who had also been the star witness at the Rivonia trial of Nelson Mandela and the other leaders who received life sentences. Bruno had emerged as the darling of the Special Branch and had given his evidence, as if from a photographic memory, with the 'swaggering arrogance and self-confidence of the old lag who knows the ropes', in the words of Joel Joffe.[*] The defence was able to establish that he had been a recidivist criminal whose speciality had been breaking into railway property.

Rusty Bernstein had been found not guilty in the Rivonia trial, after which he and Hilda fled the country. They passed through Dar es Salaam on their way to London and Hilda conveyed Bram Fischer's fond regards to Eleanor with a comment that she had been correct, from the start, about Mtolo's treachery.

Eleanor's face turned sombre as she came to the most distressing news. Babla Saloojee had been detained in the course of the year and had 'fallen' to his death from the seventh floor of Security Police headquarters in Johannesburg, while being 'interviewed' about his activities. It was patently clear that he had been tortured to death – one of a growing number of such victims, who the SB explained had died because

* Joel Joffe, *The State vs Nelson Mandela*, 2007, p. 91.

they had 'slipped on soap', jumped to their deaths or hanged themselves in their cells.

Eleanor also told Ronnie her mother's words regarding Brigid, the strain and despair evident on her face. They both felt helpless but were disinclined to wallow in their depression. At the end of the day, they reluctantly parted company, unsure when and where they would meet again. There was the possibility that he would be sent home to rejoin the underground. If so, he promised her, he would find Brigid this time and whisk her out of the country. It sounded like a romantic gesture, but at least it gave Eleanor something to dream about.

The following weeks dragged by for Eleanor and she could scarcely keep her mind on her work. She had learnt that Ronnie's group had been transferred to the main ANC base camp at Kongwa, hundreds of kilometres into the interior. After a month Duma Nokwe gave her the news that Oliver Tambo would be sending for Ronnie and Chris Hani to work on a secret research programme in Dar es Salaam. What was more, he would be allowed to live with her at the ANC residence. This was a ramshackle house in a palm grove outside the city centre. Moses Kotane and Mark Shope, the trade union leader, as well as two recent arrivals from home, Reg and Hetty September, lived there with some of the staff members. Eleanor, who shared a room with another woman, was given permission to use an outhouse for Ronnie and herself. He arrived the following day, and the two painted the room white, placed mosquito netting on the windows, and furnished it with the necessary bed, table and chairs from ANC stores. It was very pleasant, private and deliciously cool under the palm trees. They could not have been happier and considered themselves extremely fortunate.

Duma was the leader always assigned to talk with them. 'We've got a bit of a problem,' he announced as they sat on his balcony across the road from the ANC office. 'There are complaints from one or two of our Mother Grundys, who are saying it's not right that the two of you are living together but are not married.' The statement had the tone of a question, as though Duma was placing the ball in their court.

Ronnie's response was immediate. 'If Eleanor will agree to marry me, and the ANC allows it, comrade Duma, we'll end our wicked ways and make our relationship legal.' So it was agreed, and Eleanor was thrilled. She immediately removed the gold wedding ring on her finger that she had been given 'the first time round', as she put it, and arranged for it to be recast by a local goldsmith. Ronnie would have a ring to marry her with.

At first the registrar, a quintessential English mandarin, serving out the last days of his contract, refused point-blank to allow the marriage to go ahead, because they did not have their divorce papers with them. Eleanor knew the attorney-general, who promptly wrote the official a curt note, ordering him 'to stop being obstructive, and to immediately give permission'.

The marriage ceremony was a simple affair at the Ilala Boma registry office with a cheerful Tanzanian presiding. Eleanor's hair had been styled for the first time since she left South Africa and the comrades from the office quipped that she looked like a 'European lady'. She wore a simple blue dress and carried a bouquet of flamboyant flowers. Two ANC comrades acted as witnesses: Maud Manyosi and Flag Boshielo, who was Tambo's driver.

165

Eleanor on her wedding day, December 1964.

There was a small party in Mandy and Agnes Msimang's flat opposite the ANC office. Tambo had told Agnes that 'the children are getting married, they deserve a celebration'. He himself was strictly teetotal and frowned on drink but instructed her to 'get some of the bubbly wine' for the formal toast. Tambo asked J.B. Marks to make a speech. It was full of humour and wisdom. In it he said, in a parody of the MK Manifesto ('the time comes in the life of any nation when there are only two choices: to submit or fight'), 'The time comes in any man's life to stop being indecisive and to seize the lioness lurking in the forest by the tail.' As they raised glasses filled with Tambo's 'bubbly wine', Uncle J.B. wished them the best of luck, good health and happiness in their union and said, paying tribute to the bride, 'And you dear Eleanor, our daughter, who would have thought that someone with your

166

unassuming, lady-like nature and slender frame would prove to have the strength of the lioness and vanquish the enemy? As the saying goes: touch a woman and you strike a rock!'

That night under the brilliant southern stars, with the warm Indian Ocean waves embracing the Tanzanian shore, by a simple fisherman's hut they had rented for their honeymoon, they recited Robbie Burns's poem, as their wedding vow:

Till all the seas run dry, my dear,
And the rocks melt with the sun
And I will love thee still, my dear,
While the sands of life shall run.

Appendix

In Memoriam[*]
Eleanor Janette Margaret Kasrils
9 March 1936 – 8 November 2009

My wife of forty-five years, Eleanor Kasrils, who famously escaped from South African police custody in 1963, was unassuming and modest to a fault. She would have been among the last to believe she merited an obituary in the London *Guardian*, let alone much of the South African press, which referred to her as 'a staggeringly courageous woman ... who will not be forgotten'. Neither would she have expected a memorial of the magnitude that took place in Cape Town and London to celebrate her life, with moving tributes from President Jacob Zuma and former President Thabo Mbeki and messages from Algeria, America, Britain, China, Cuba, Holland, Palestine, Russia, Scotland, and Ireland.

She was a naturally kind person with no pretensions and never sought the limelight. She was elegant and refined in her manner and it was my privilege to share a life-time's relationship with her.

---

[*] Based on a eulogy delivered by Ronnie Kasrils at memorial services in Cape Town, on 14 November 2009, and at South Africa House, London, on 14 December 2009.

President Zuma's words recalled a woman of principle who 'demonstrated great bravery, resourcefulness and initiative ... resolute in her commitment to the people of South Africa and to the cause of freedom everywhere'. Former President Mbeki wrote: 'as she moved among us with an easy grace, she carried no megaphone to broadcast a message of self-praise, nor any banner to proclaim that she had courageously dedicated her life to serve the people. Quietly, without shouting from the mountain tops, she elected not to walk along the cool sequestered vale of life, but to take the dangerous road of opposition to tyranny and the suppression of the apartheid crime against humanity.'

A young Palestine Solidarity activist who attended the memorial service in Cape Town and who, like Eleanor, had studied and loved art, offered the following observation: 'Whilst sitting in the service, listening to the speakers – all of whom seemed to reflect different dimensions of Eleanor's life – and looking at the wonderful photographs of Eleanor, I thought, Eleanor's life *itself* is her masterpiece – a true work of art. And it will live on in every person she has touched along the way.'

Eleanor would have been surprised by the outpourings of love and affection which so many friends from all over the world have conveyed. Such tributes have greatly fortified us as a family. It was fitting to have a memorial service in London, the place where Eleanor lived as an exile for over 26 years, from 1965 to 1991, for all that time in a modest, low-budget apartment off a narrow service lane in Golders Green. She resided there longer than anywhere else, including Durban, where she grew up.

170

The memorial events have been extremely moving and inevitably sad and bitter-sweet; for with the agony of her passing there have come acknowledgements of a life rich in joy and fulfilment with uplifting and inspiring memories. The photographic slide-show was lovingly put together by our son Andrew with musical selections which Eleanor – a person whose home was filled with melody and flowers – adored.

With respect to the musicians featured, she had met Pete Seeger in Dar es Salaam in 1964 and took him to the ANC office to perform for the comrades. His 'If I had a hammer' became something of an anthem for the ANC and Eleanor admired its simple call for love, freedom and justice. When she worked as a geology technician at South London College in 1973, a jazz musician colleague roped her in to help stage a tour for the legendary Sonny Terry and Brownie McGhee from America's Deep South, whose 'God and man' became one of the atheistical Eleanor's favourites. On hearing this played at our secular memorial meeting in Cape Town, Archbishop Desmond Tutu beamed with sheer delight.

As regards some of the other music played, we danced cheek-to-cheek to Ella Fitzgerald's 'Our love is here to stay' from the early days of our passion way back in the Durban of 1961 to, most recently, the quiet of the evenings following my retirement from government in our new home overlooking the grandeur of False Bay, near Cape Town. Robbie Burns's 'My love is like a red, red rose' was our best-loved poem. She was of course a Scottish lassie who came to South Africa as an infant – one of Scotland's 'finest exports' as Brian Filling, of Scottish Anti-Apartheid, has reminded us. Her father and the male lineage on both parents' side were Kilmarnock engineers, who came out of working-class apprenticeship as fitters-and-turners and boilermakers. Her maternal uncle, Jack MacDonald, was a fighter pilot killed in action in 1943. This stood us in great stead when Joe Modise, former commander of the ANC's military wing, asked me to propose a toast to the South African Air Force at a banquet in Pretoria in 1993, prior to South Africa's first democratic election and before the amalgamation of our armed forces. Rising next to my elegant wife and mentioning that her uncle had been a pilot in the RAF soon put paid to their nightmares about having to work with 'terrorists' such as Joe Modise and Red Ron.

Eleanor explained her Scots background to Hilda Bernstein in a 1990 interview: 'My father ... went to Scotland [in 1935] to serve an apprenticeship. He met my mother there. They returned to South Africa just before the war when I was six months old. I never knew myself as being Scottish, but always South African. And now there's this anomaly: I've got a British passport, and it says "Born in Scotland". But in fact I am South African.'*

Eleanor was influenced by the works of Robbie Burns, by such lines of his as 'countless mortals mourn man's inhumanity to man'. She had an abiding sense of what was right and wrong and the need to stand up for justice and the poor – which was why she loved Pete Seeger's hammer song. As a dutiful daughter growing up in Durban, under rather tight parental control, she enjoyed the artistic leftish circles her parents then moved in, which fed her curiosity about life's magic. Among other pursuits she loved to go fishing with her

* Hilda Bernstein, *The Rift: The Exile Experience of South Africans*, 1994.

172

father. She would adroitly bait the hooks and learnt many skills from him. After the Sharpeville massacre of March 1960, and a divorce from a claustrophobic marriage, she exulted in a new-found freedom she had never experienced in her life and joined the fight for justice, equality and democracy in South Africa. Eleanor was soon defying the apartheid state in protest demonstrations and joined the ANC-aligned Congress of Democrats and outlawed Communist Party after having been close to the Liberal Party. She became one of the first women recruited into the ANC's military wing, Umkhonto weSizwe (Spear of the Nation, or MK for short) and served with courage and distinction.

Her fellow activist Ebrahim Ismail Ebrahim (an ex–Robben Island prisoner and currently South Africa's deputy foreign minister) recollects Eleanor's contribution during those turbulent times: 'I knew Eleanor from 1960 when she was a young revolutionary activist in Durban. I have fond memories of participating with her in many public demonstrations. It was a time when the ANC was banned and the apartheid regime was determined to destroy all forms of resistance. Eleanor worked for a large book firm and was of great assistance to the underground, often using the bookshop for clandestine messages. She was our contact point. Even in the most difficult of times she had a fantastic sense of humour, and for many of us who lived underground, being hunted by the security police, she was a great source of inspiration. She never lost her discipline, and her commitment to the liberation of South Africa never wavered.'

Eleanor bravely shouldered many roles from trade unionist to combatant and activist, but additionally she was something of a secret agent linking underground structures at a most difficult phase of the struggle during the Rivonia arrests in 1963. She secretly liaised with Bram Fischer, Hilda Bernstein and the remnants of the underground, taking huge risks to keep the fugitives supplied with funds, information and instructions. When I was appointed Minister for Intelligence Services in 2004, and Eleanor and I met the staff, I introduced her as 'a far more successful secret agent than I had ever been because she was so discreet and understated – a perfect operative in the Le Carré mould'.

Eleanor was one of that rare breed of white South Africans who were willing to give up the privilege of their colour and background and had the courage to opt for active struggle. This was despite the fact that she was a divorced, single parent with a young daughter from a marriage which she entered into when she was only nineteen and which she soon discovered had been a grave mistake. The ANC leader Pallo Jordan referred to Eleanor as 'a human being who could not stand by' as apartheid destroyed her country and its disenfranchised people. South Africa today would be a different place indeed if the Eleanors of this world had opted for personal security, ease and privilege and simply the wringing of hands in the face of tyranny.

She was most protective of her daughter Brigid and did everything she possibly could to shield her from danger. She was able to utilise the convenient presence of her parents to assist with caring for her young child when she was arrested in 1963, and placed her trust in them. A rift opened between them and their 'communist' daughter after her daring escape from custody and flight across the border into exile. Eleanor's expectation that her parents would send her daughter to join her was not to be, and it was another twelve years before she was finally reunited with Brigid in London. That separation had been an agony for her. Hilda Bernstein carefully chose the term 'rift' for the title of her book about the pain of exile.

Much has been written and spoken about Eleanor's arrest in 1963 and the manner of her daring escape. A young friend has written about how she got Eleanor to talk of that experience. Eleanor did so 'without a hint of bravado, as if anyone could have arranged such an escape,' she wrote, and continued, 'She seemed to feel that her own role in the struggle, and the years of support for Ronnie and the children (in London from 1965 onwards), hardly merited a mention.'

There are endearing anecdotes about Eleanor which illustrate her wit, verve and delight in life, qualities she maintained to the end. It is a huge testament to her inner strength and will that she remained staunch and true to her principles and commitment through the decades. While she kept the family together through love and hard work, uncomplainingly enduring many years of privation and domestic grind in exile, imprinting on her young sons Andrew and Christopher the shining values they possess (articulated in their moving tributes to their mother), she found time to teach a younger generation of revolutionaries the skills of clandestine work and disguise.

In 1988 she was accused by a Tory MP, who was close to the South African Security Police, of 'recruiting and training terrorists' from her Golders Green home in London. She became aware of his accusation, against her and others, while at lunch in a London pub near her work, noting the newspaper headlines over a stranger's shoulder. This ran: 'MP Names London Terror Cell'.* The MP called on the British Home Secretary 'to consider deportations', but when she challenged him to make his statements outside Parliament he backed off.

She had indeed continued with her quiet, behind-the-scenes role of assisting the outlawed liberation movement from exile, but this was never the work of 'terrorism' as the apartheid regime and the Tory MP alleged. Even under the threat of spies and surveillance, and the dangers that dogged her no less than others, she managed somehow to find the precious time, while working as a chief technician and administrator in London educational institutes, to continue to take risks for the cause. Few in the liberation movement were aware of this fact or the huge personal sacrifices that were entailed. The threat from South Africa's security services and spies was ever-present, so much so that Scotland Yard was on occasions called in to inspect suspicious-looking packages delivered to the front door of her home. Information later emerged that an assassin had been dispatched to try and kill Pallo Jordan and me with a poisoned umbrella. One day in 1970 we received a cutting from a South African newspaper reporting that Eleanor's old Nemesis, Lieutenant Grobler, had blown his brains out in his Durban home. The story reported that he had distinguished himself in the fight against 'terrorism' in South Africa and Namibia, but his single failure related to Eleanor's escape.

Her comrade and fellow underground worker Bill Anderson has provided a unique portrait of Eleanor the secret agent which is worth quoting.

* *Evening Standard*, 3 November 1988.

'The obituaries to Eleanor have spoken of her courage and loyalty in the early years of MK. I would like to place firmly on the record the role that Eleanor played for three whole decades in the ranks of MK.

'Throughout the years of exile London was an important sphere of the underground struggle. It provided a range of services, technologies and resources that were hard to come by in the forward areas. And despite the political space provided by the Anti-Apartheid Movement, it was not always friendly terrain. It required operatives who were credible, discreet and professional. Eleanor was one of the best.

'Communications between the forward areas and South Africa were often treacherous. Eleanor provided an array of relays: public phone boxes, safe postal addresses, clean couriers. And in moments of crisis, as when an operational unit faced meltdown, Eleanor was there: to calmly patch links together between the comrades in the field and their commanders in the rear.

'In matters of disguise she was an expert. Where do you find a wig for an African that won't make him look like Shaft? Where can you buy a priest's cassock and dog-collar? And what kind of questions are they going to ask you in this very proper shop in the back streets of Victoria?

'Sophisticated surveillance technology went commercial in the eighties. Eleanor not only knew her way round the catalogues. She discovered a string of gadget shops on the Edgware Road that were as good as the posh establishments of Mayfair. And a whole lot safer.

'Eleanor was a supremely good people-person. She had a particular ability – a mix of the personal and political – to recruit non–South African sympathisers into the struggle, and to persuade them to do some pretty brave things, not only from abroad but inside South Africa as well. Safe houses, couriers, reconnaissance missions: Eleanor handled them all.

'So how does one assess Eleanor's role?

'It is possible to paint a picture of Eleanor as loyal mother, wife and comrade, earning a living, looking after home and family – with Ronnie away at the front – and helping out whenever she could. This is indeed true, but insufficient.

'To the extent that the ANC was, for thirty years, dependent on its underground structures to keep the movement alive, and to the extent that the underground, operating primarily in an urban terrain, required a multifaceted technical infrastructure to survive, it was people like Eleanor who provided one indispensable part of the skeleton on which the political body flourished. In this role she was a true professional, and, judged as such, she emerges with flying colours.'

Working for the ANC in exile and later in government as wife of an activist and then a minister was no bed of roses and entailed much hard work and responsibility. Eleanor had worked in the Dar es Salaam office for the ANC during 1963–5 and was singled out to assist ANC President Oliver Tambo with his papers after he returned to South Africa in 1991, until his death in 1993.

She was constantly and loyally at my side when I became a minister in the new democratic government from 1994 to 2008. She was an outstanding representative of South Africa on ministerial visits abroad or when needing to entertain important guests at home. She never failed to impress with her easy-going charm and cultural knowledge and pursuits.

She made life-long friendships across the international divide – East and West – with government representatives and popular movements alike, as the tributes received attest. So many simply referred to her as 'Lady Eleanor', so struck were they by her poise and refinement.

Her personal kindness has been much referred to. A female government official whom she befriended wrote that she 'was always there supporting Ronnie, a quiet but powerful force in the life of the Department of Water Affairs' where I was minister. Eleanor's caring touch is remarked upon by the same friend: 'I still have a precious little orchid that Eleanor bought for me at a street market in Bali during the negotiations in the run-up to the World Summit on Sustainable Development, knowing how much I like orchids. That generosity of spirit and her irreverent spirit that brought the orchid back home, I will always carry with me.'

Eleanor was a true, dear friend to so many. The perception some may have had of her initial reserve was generally regarded as shyness or even a slight aloofness. But this was rather because she never rushed into making hasty, impulsive decisions or friendships. She needed the space to decide whether she could trust new acquaintances. Where she felt at ease, a natural rapport would flow. Where she found rudeness or arrogance, she simply switched off.

It is thought that revolutionaries have to combine the qualities of both love and ruthlessness, comparable to the metaphors of flowers and stone – soft and beautiful yet at the same time hard and tough. She was certainly as diaphanous as daffodils but never harsh and unfeeling. She was like bamboo – with the suppleness and strength of that lithe plant – capable of riding out the fiercest and most prolonged of storms. That was the strength she shared with her African sisters, best exemplified in the declaration of the ANC Women's League: 'Once you have touched a woman, you have struck a rock.'

A young friend of our sons, who played with them in our Golders Green home in the 1970s, and is now a university lecturer, has written: 'I remember Eleanor as a warm and funny adult, one of the fixed points of kindness in our child's-eye view of the world. It is extraordinary to learn that she managed to be all those things while also pursuing a political vision with such commitment. It makes me think of something I have just been teaching. W.B. Yeats has a line about the woman he was in love with, regretting the way her commitment to revolutionary politics had hardened her ('Too long a sacrifice can make a stone of the heart'). Now, whenever I read that line, I think of Eleanor and know that it isn't inevitable.'

The same writer remembers how Eleanor provided a lunch of hot dogs and assured him that she had specially bought kosher sausages for him. He comments: 'What an extraordinary thing for a revolutionary communist to bother over. It suggests a kindness of humanity, a generosity, where you might expect to find revolutionary intolerance.'

So many friends have remembered Eleanor in touching ways. A Durban struggle veteran from the 1960s, Eric Singh, writes: 'If looks can deceive, then that person was Eleanor. For the stranger it would be difficult to believe that this quiet-spoken, dainty woman had the heart of a lion, with guts unlimited.' Magdalene Louw, our housekeeper in government residence, paying tribute at the Cape Town memorial service, said: 'Thank you, Eleanor, for everything you have done for me. Since the first day I worked for you in 1994, I appreciated your fairness. Sometimes without saying a word, but seeing you with a beautiful smile made me feel comfortable. You were my doctor when I was sick. You were my psychologist when I felt depressed. You were my financial adviser when I struggled. You were my life-saver when my problems became too much. I never regret sharing my confidential life with you. I always knew you were there to help me. Oh, my special days with you!'

From Ireland, Declan Kearney of Sinn Fein wrote: 'As we exchanged hugs and goodbyes outside historic Kilmainham Gaol, Dublin, in February 2007, Ronnie said, "We are family now." We think fond memories of Eleanor … a lovely woman with whom we really connected. We will always recall that evening in Dublin when we dined, drank, laughed and danced, and you and Eleanor led the way. And then, how we all stood and watched the lunar eclipse. Now Eleanor has become one of the beacon stars in the sky to guide us all.'

Sybilla Higgs, who worked with Eleanor in the Durban bookshop in the early 1960s, has written: 'I first met Eleanor when I was 16 and just out of boarding school; she was an elegant, independent, vivacious role model. She was partly responsible for introducing me to some of the most important influences in my life: not only books – I worked with her in her mother's bookshop where I began to establish my passion for reading – but also political belief, the importance of equality and justice and those who were prepared to risk their lives for it. And it was also Eleanor who introduced me to my husband, Barry, who changed my life. There are also memories of the time we lived together in Golders Green, filled with the joys and tribulations of pregnancies and babies. More recently Eleanor wrote to me about her delight in her new garden and the views across False Bay from the house in St James. I replied saying: I hope that you and Ronnie will now at last find time to walk hand in hand along the beach.'

Eleanor was a revolutionary: courageous, principled and of high moral integrity who gave up her own security and privilege to fight for freedom and justice for the oppressed. This she did without any thought of gaining high position or reward. She suffered immeasurably in the process, as a very vulnerable mother, from the long estrangement from her daughter, Brigid. Yet Eleanor came to reconcile with her parents, which for them was made easier by the ANC's rise to power, vindicating the choice she had made. Back in South Africa after 1991 she affectionately nursed them both through long periods of illness before they died. She loved her children and did everything she could for them. As President Zuma stated: 'She was the glue that held her family together. She had to overcome the hardships of separation, uncertainty and insecurity. She did so with grace and resolve, without complaint or self-pity.'

Despite those times, including the many years of living apart from me when I was deployed in southern Africa, our relationship managed to deepen and mature. It was indeed a joyous and privileged bond of affection that lasted 48 years – not the fortune of many couples. When death came – as it must come to us all – it crept in suddenly, like a thief in the night. She had been under the surgeon's knife more than once and she bore the scars, the aftermath, the constant medication bravely and stoically. Mercifully, the massive stroke that smote her took her life swiftly, within a matter of hours. The preceding days had seen her in delightful spirit. We had taken our favourite walk along the coastal shore, where the whales visit to calve in spring, down to the small fishing harbour, hand in hand like a pair of young lovers, delighting in a wonderful sunlit day that tinged, as ever, her limpid grey eyes with a blue sparkle. We sat at our favourite restaurant sipping chilled wine and eating freshly caught fish and watched the fishing boats come in and the sun set over the magnificent bay where we had made our home. Everyone who knew her, and had seen her in the previous weeks, remarked how happy she looked. This they have as their abiding memory of her, and of the two of us together.

Birth and death are the book-ends of a life that can encase few or many chapters; eventful or mundane, heroic or apathetic, significant or trivial. Eleanor's life-span was 73 years, and the episodes that made up her life are truly amazing in their relevance and value: for us as a family, for her many friends, for the people of South Africa, for the international community. This was a remarkable woman, whose ashes merge with the indigenous assegai tree, so symbolic of the ANC and MK, which we planted in Kirstenbosch Gardens.

She was indeed a lovely human being for whom it can be said: 'she never lacked appreciation of earth's beauty or failed to express it; she looked for the best in others and gave the best she had.' May I add these words from Conrad Aiken: 'gently they go, the beautiful, the tender, the kind; quietly they go, the intelligent, the witty, the brave.' As one friend wrote to me, 'Eleanor embodied all these attributes.'